THE ILLUSTRATED HISTORY OF
THE INCAS

THE ILLUSTRATED HISTORY OF
THE INCAS

The extraordinary story of the lost world of the Andes, chronicling the ancient civilizations of the Paracas, Chavín, Nazca and Moche, and other tribes and cultures of ancient South America

Fully illustrated throughout with over 200 photographs of sites, sculptures, ceramics and artefacts, and with fine art paintings, maps, plans and cutaway drawings

David M Jones

southwater

I would like to dedicate this book to my wife Anne, daughter Megan and son Sam.

This edition is published by Southwater, an imprint of Anness Publishing Ltd, Hermes House, 88–89 Blackfriars Road, London SE1 8HA tel. 020 7401 2077; fax 020 7633 9499

www.southwaterbooks.com; www.annesspublishing.com

Anness Publishing has a new picture agency outlet for images for publishing, promotions or advertising. Please visit our website www.practicalpictures.com for more information.

UK agent: The Manning Partnership Ltd;
    tel. 01225 478444; fax 01225 478440; sales@manning-partnership.co.uk
UK distributor: Grantham Book Services Ltd
    tel. 01476 541080; fax 01476 541061; orders@gbs.tbs-ltd.co.uk
North American agent/distributor: National Book Network
    tel. 301 459 3366; fax 301 429 5746; www.nbnbooks.com
Australian agent/distributor: Pan Macmillan Australia
    tel. 1300 135 113; fax 1300 135 103; customer.service@macmillan.com.au
New Zealand agent/distributor: David Bateman Ltd
    tel. (09) 415 7664; fax (09) 415 8892

Publisher: Joanna Lorenz
Senior Managing Editor: Conor Kilgallon
Editor: Joy Wotton
Designers: Nigel Partridge and Adelle Morris
Illustrators: Anthony Duke, Rob Highton and Vanessa Card
Editorial Reader: Lindsay Zamponi
Production Controller: Steve Lang

Ethical Trading Policy
At Anness Publishing we believe that business should be conducted in an ethical and ecologically sustainable way, with respect for the environment and a proper regard to the replacement of the natural resources we employ.
    As a publisher, we use a lot of wood pulp to make high-quality paper for printing, and that wood commonly comes from spruce trees. We are therefore currently growing more than 500,000 trees in two Scottish forest plantations near Aberdeen – Berrymoss (130 hectares/320 acres) and West Touxhill (125 hectares/305 acres). The forests we manage contain twice the number of trees employed each year in paper-making for our books.
    Because of this ongoing ecological investment programme, you, as our customer, can have the pleasure and reassurance of knowing that a tree is being cultivated on your behalf to naturally replace the materials used to make the book you are holding.
    Our forestry programme is run in accordance with the UK Woodland Assurance Scheme (UKWAS) and will be certified by the internationally recognized Forest Stewardship Council (FSC). The FSC is a non-government organization dedicated to promoting responsible management of the world's forests. Certification ensures forests are managed in an environmentally sustainable and socially responsible way. For further information about this scheme, go to www.annesspublishing.com/trees

© Anness Publishing Ltd 2007`

Previously published as part of a larger volume, *The Illustrated Encyclopedia of the Incas*

Front cover main image shows: painted Chimú textile depicting a shaman in a trance, surrounded by snarling felines, serpents and birds. Page 1: Inca Trail, Peru. Page 2: Torréon temple at Machu Picchu. page 3: Huayna Picchu overlooking Machu Picchu. Page 4, from left: approach to Machu Picchu; remains of Muyu Marca Tower. Page 5, from left: the Inca Trail; black llamas; ancient Inca sentry post of Runkuraqay; external view of Sacsayhuaman.

CONTENTS

Introduction   6
An Ancient Civilization   8

Discovering the Incas and
    Their Past   **10**
The Spanish Explorations   12
Chroniclers and Informants   14
Languages, Drawings and *Quipu*   16
Explorers and Archaeologists   18
Modern Investigations   20
Timeline: The Incas and Their
    Ancestors   22

Empire of the Sun   **26**
Land of the Four Quarters   28
Cuzco and Beyond   30
Building an Empire   32
Civil War   34
Conquest of the Empire   36
Capture and Regicide   38

The Land   **40**

Peaks and Mountain Valleys   42

Abundant Plains – the Altiplano   44

Western Deserts and Coastal Valleys   46

The *Montaña* and Eastern Rainforests   48

Land of Extremes   50

Living Within the Landscape   52

Sacred Landscapes, Sacred Skies   **54**

Places of Worship   56

Sacred Waters   58

Mountains of the Gods   60

Lines in the Desert   62

Ceque Pathways   64

Religion and Trade   66

Cosmos and Galaxy   68

Heavenly Constellations   70

Early Settlers to Empire Builders   **72**

The First Arrivals   74

Developing Communities   76

New Agriculture and Architecture   78

Oracle and Shrine: Chavín de Huántar   80

Southern Cults: Paracas and Pukará   82

Nazca Confederacy and Moche State   84

Mountain Empires: Wari and Tiwanaku   86

Kingdoms and Shrines   88

Conquest and Empire: the Incas   90

Themes and Peoples   **92**

Civic-Ceremonial Centres   94

Communal Ritual: Kotosh   96

Exchange of Goods and Ideas   98

Conflict and Co-operation   100

Religious Cohesion   102

Peoples of the Empire   104

Power and Warfare   **106**

The Nazca Confederacy   108

The Moche State   110

The Empire of Tiwanaku   112

The Wari Empire   114

The Kingdom of Chimú   116

The Inca Empire   118

Politics of Empire   120

Social Organization   122

Glossary   124

Index   125

Picture Acknowledgements   128

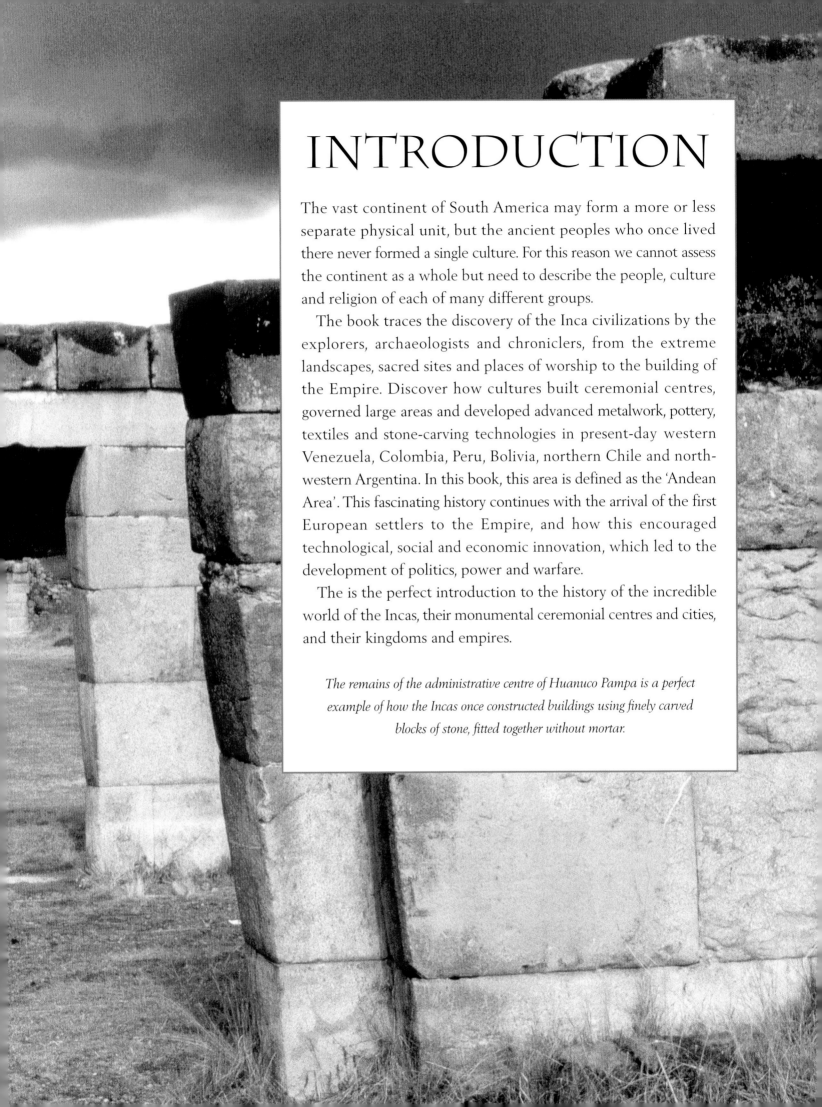

INTRODUCTION

The vast continent of South America may form a more or less separate physical unit, but the ancient peoples who once lived there never formed a single culture. For this reason we cannot assess the continent as a whole but need to describe the people, culture and religion of each of many different groups.

The book traces the discovery of the Inca civilizations by the explorers, archaeologists and chroniclers, from the extreme landscapes, sacred sites and places of worship to the building of the Empire. Discover how cultures built ceremonial centres, governed large areas and developed advanced metalwork, pottery, textiles and stone-carving technologies in present-day western Venezuela, Colombia, Peru, Bolivia, northern Chile and north-western Argentina. In this book, this area is defined as the 'Andean Area'. This fascinating history continues with the arrival of the first European settlers to the Empire, and how this encouraged technological, social and economic innovation, which led to the development of politics, power and warfare.

The is the perfect introduction to the history of the incredible world of the Incas, their monumental ceremonial centres and cities, and their kingdoms and empires.

The remains of the administrative centre of Huanuco Pampa is a perfect example of how the Incas once constructed buildings using finely carved blocks of stone, fitted together without mortar.

AN ANCIENT CIVILIZATION

When Francisco Pizarro and the Spanish conquistadors arrived in the Andes in 1532 they found a civilization of great sophistication and wealth. Well-planned cities with storehouses and complex ceremonial architecture, irrigated lands and an established system of agriculture, transport and communication routes, and an organized, hierarchical society were all signs of an intelligent and civilized people. Starting from the Cuzco Valley, the Incas had gradually expanded their power to form an empire, conquering and integrating land and settlements from the coastal plains inland to the rainforest. From its early roots it had developed from small farming villages to large cities with sophisticated forms of organization.

Below: A Middle Horizon bridge-spout effigy vessel from Tiwanaku with distinctive jaguar coat. Jaguars were revered by sierra cultures.

Yet despite these momentous achievements, the Incas' reign lasted less than 100 years. To understand how the Incas rose from around 40,000 people to form the largest empire in South America, we need to understand the land they lived in, their way of life, their conquests and spread of influence and, perhaps more than anything else, their religion and myths, for these lay behind so many aspects of Inca life and influenced everything from agriculture to temple building.

ANDEAN CIVILIZATION

South America comprises many dramatically different geological areas. From high Altiplanos to low coastal valleys, from lush, dense rainforest to dry, barren deserts, each landscape offers different rewards and challenges and shapes the lifestyles of its inhabitants. Such differences, and the geographical isolation of many settlements, led to different peoples in South America developing at different paces. At the same time, however, cultures in various large areas were aware of each other, and they developed links through trade, political alliance, conquest and the diffusion of ideas through direct or indirect contact.

Ancient South American cultures that can be described as 'civilizations' were confined to the Andes mountains and nearby western coastal valleys and deserts. Elsewhere, South American peoples did develop quite sophisticated societies and beliefs.

Above: Descending the Inca Trail from the Second Pass, the walker approaches the ridge-top ruins of the Sayaqmarka compound.

However, they did not build monumental ceremonial centres or cities, or develop technology of quite the same level of complexity as the Andean kingdoms and empires, and are therefore not defined as 'civilizations'.

This book concentrates on the 'Andean Area', where civilizations evolved in the sierras and adjacent foothills and coastal regions, north to south from the Colombian–Ecuadorian border to the northern half of Chile and east to west from the Amazonian Rainforest to the Pacific coast. City-states, kingdoms and empires evolved in this area, based on maize and potato agriculture and the herding of llamas, alpacas and vicuñas. The concentration of civilization in the Andean Area was due in part to the geography of the region. Within a relatively small area there is a range of contrasting landscapes, from Pacific ocean-bound coastal plains and deserts, to coastal and foothill valleys, to high mountain valleys and plateaux, to the eastern slopes running down to the edges of the rainforests and high pampas of Argentina.

A key factor in the development and endurance of these civilizations was access to and control of water, which became

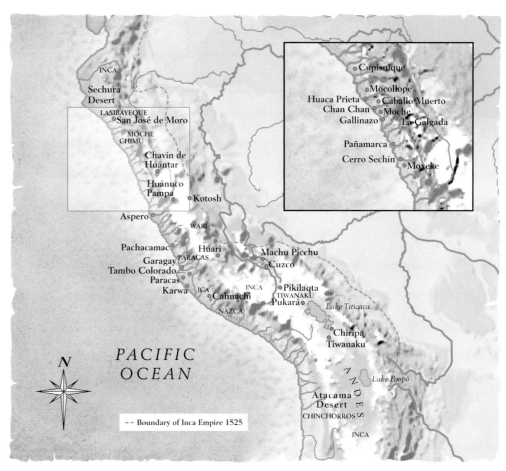

important not only functionally but also symbolically and religiously. Water was essential for agriculture, and people in naturally dry regions developed a sophisticated form of agriculture based on complex irrigation technologies, often combined with land terracing. As a result, a wide variety of crops was grown in both lowland and highland regions, which led to the development of trade between the two. The development of agriculture and trade led to different cultures specializing in different products – and not only essentials such as food but increasingly non-essential items such as ceramics and items with religious significance. As a result, these cultures developed into complex and orderly societies with sophisticated religious beliefs and structures. Thus empires are born.

SOURCES OF INFORMATION

Our knowledge of the Incas (and other South American peoples) comes from a variety of sources: from the Inca record-keepers themselves (both the *amautas* and

Below: Reed fishing boats and huts on Lake Titicaca, between Peru and Bolivia. Such vessels and materials are still used today.

the *quipucamayoqs*), from contemporary Spanish accounts and from archaeological investigations, both recent and in the past. All give us fascinating insights into a rich and colourful civilization with legendary rulers, a civil war, sacred places, mystical lines and images in the desert, imposing temples and evocative symbols, and a literal belief that the Incas will one day return to power.

REMAINS OF EMPIRES

The buildings constructed by the cult of Chávin de Huántar in the Early Horizon, the Wari and Tiwanaku empires in the Middle Horizon and the Incas in the Late Horizon can be seen and marvelled at today, along with other remains from the Andean Area. Such remains help us to understand the architectural and engineering skills of the various peoples, their social organization, their main forms of occupation and trade, and their religions.

Chávin de Huántar was a pilgrimage centre, established *c.*900BC as a U-shaped centre (others include La Galgada and Sechín Alto, both built in the Preceramic Period). Its remains show a labyrinth of passages and galleries.

Above: General map of the Inca Empire and important sites, showing how the empire stretched the length of the Andes Mountains.

Other fantastic pre-Inca sites are the Gateway of the Sun at the Tiwanaku Akapana Temple; the Paracas Cavernas cemetery, known for its desiccated mummies; the Moche centre of Cerro Blanco, where two large ceremonial platforms – the Huacas del Sol and de la Luna – were built; and the Late Intermediate Period Chimú city of Chan Chan, which comprised a complex of compounds (*ciudadelas*) containing residences for the reigning king and earlier deceased kings.

Famous remains from the Incas themselves include the city of Cuzco, the 'navel of the world', rebuilt in the plan of a crouching puma, and site of the Coricancha Temple; Huánuco Pampa, a seat of provincial admininstration; and the dramatically sited hilltop sacred city of Machu Picchu, a massive landmark on the Inca Trail. In addition, Inca engineers constructed an impressive array of roads and bridges, as well as enabling land to be developed for farming through the construction of terraces and irrigation canals.

DISCOVERING THE INCAS AND THEIR PAST

Unlike many other ancient civilizations worldwide, none of the Andean peoples invented an alphabet or any other form of writing. As a result, the first accounts of any ancient Andean culture or history were written by Spanish conquistadors, then later by 16th- and 17th-century Spanish chroniclers.

The conquistadors related what they observed on discovering the Incas, while later chroniclers recorded accounts of the empire, its people and culture. They used two sources of information for their records: *quipucamayoqs* and *amautas*. The first were people who devised the 'writing' system of knots known as *quipus*, which involved coloured cords tied into bundles with knots, while the second were court historians responsible for learning and relating details of their culture. Interpreting these accounts was not aided by the fact that many hundreds of languages and dialects existed at that time, although one language, Quechua, dominated.

During the 19th century, more was learned about Inca and pre-Inca civilizations from the studies and collections carried out by explorers and naturalists in the earliest excavations. Further additions to our knowledge come from the results and interpretations of 20th- and 21st-century archaeological discoveries, including that of the Inca sacred city of Machu Picchu.

Left: Shadows and light on the walls of the Sacsahuaman temple mimic the lighting on the sacred landscape that lies behind it.

THE SPANISH EXPLORATIONS

Europeans first discovered the New World ('Vinland') as early as AD986, although at that time they were unaware of the vastness of its lands. However, the settlement made there was all but forgotten by Europeans by the time Christopher Columbus and others began to explore across the Atlantic in the late 15th and early 16th centuries.

THE ARRIVAL OF THE SPANISH

After explorations from Hispaniola (modern Haiti and the Dominican Republic), during 1504–9, Spaniards established the first permanent occupation of Tierra Firme (the South American mainland) in Panama in 1509. From the isthmus, Francisco Pizarro and others explored and eventually conquered the vast Inca Empire of the Andes in 1533.

Their descriptions of the peoples and cultures they found formed the opinions of Europeans towards the new worlds they had 'discovered', and enhanced convictions already formed about the natives

Below: Atahualpa, the last Inca emperor, was engaged in a bitter civil war when Pizarro landed on the northern coast of the empire.

Above: Early 16th-century Spanish caravels were the type of ships used by the explorers and conquistadors.

of the Caribbean islands. When Pizarro led his first expedition to Tierra Firme in 1524, the Aztec Empire had already been conquered by Hernán Cortés. (The reality that Columbus had not reached China but had found an unsuspected and unknown New World had become common knowledge.) Spaniards were sure that other vast empires and rich cities were there for the taking, and set out to conquer and exploit the wealth of these places for their own glory and enrichment.

With their belief that they were a superior race with a righteous duty to convert the 'heathens' they found to Christianity, to rule them and to exploit them, few Spaniards had any desire to engage with these civilizations.

A MAN WITH AMBITIONS

Pizarro made three expeditions: 1524–5, 1526–7 and 1531–3. In the first he only barely penetrated the coast of Colombia, but in the second he marched farther inland and sent his ship captain, Bartholomew Ruíz, down the coast.

Pizarro met with a mixed reception but soon began to collect gold and silver objects, and to hear tales of vast cities and riches to the south. Ruíz brought back tales of many sightings of increasing population and civilization, and no apparent hostility or fear. Moreover, he encountered a balsa trading raft well out to sea laden with gold and silver objects, elaborate textiles and two traders from the Inca subject port of Tumbes, whom he brought to Pizarro along with the gold, silver and cloth. From these two men the Spaniards learned of fabulous Inca cities, palaces, llama flocks and endless stores of gold and silver objects.

Sufficient gold and silver was taken back to Spain to whet the appetite of the Spanish crown and to interest enough adventurers to raise funds to send a third expedition, this time into the Andes, with the purpose of conquest and conversion.

The Inca Empire discovered by Pizarro was at its greatest expansion, but had only recently itself conquered the kingdoms and peoples of the northern Andes and coasts of modern Ecuador and central Colombia. Nevertheless, Pizarro's chroniclers describe vast wealth in gold and silver objects, rich textiles, neatly laid-out cities and storehouses full of produce and other goods. There were masonry walls and fortresses of blocks so well fitted together that no mortar was needed, lands with irrigation systems and sophisticated agriculture and herds of 'sheep' (llamas). Balsa rafts traded up and down the coasts, while transport and communication were facilitated by a network of smooth roads and bridges along the coasts, across rivers and into the high mountains.

SMALLPOX AND CIVIL WAR

The Spaniards also found an empire in trouble, partly, although unknowingly, of their own doing. Ironically, smallpox, introduced into mainland America by the

Below: Francisco Pizarro and Diego de Almagro, his ambitious accomplice, as depicted by Guaman Poma de Ayala.

Spaniards in their conquest of the Aztecs, spread rapidly south from Mesoamerica, infecting the last conquering Sapa Inca (emperor), Huayna Capac (1493–1526), along with his heir apparent. As he became ill, Huayna Capac received reports from traders from the northern reaches of his empire of bearded strangers who sailed in strange ships. These reports coincided with a series of ill omens, and his priests prophesied evil and disaster when they witnessed the death of an eagle, which fell out of the sky after being mobbed by buzzards, during ceremonies in honour of the sun god Inti.

When Capac died, his son Huáscar seized the throne but was challenged by another son, Atahualpa, who commanded the Inca armies and marched from the

Above: Francisco Pizarro of Trujillo, of Estremadura, Spain (1475–1541), conqueror of the Incas.

northernmost province of Quito. The Inca court split into two supporting factions and civil war raged for six years. At the time of Pizarro's arrival at Tumbes on the coast of Quito province in 1532, Atahualpa's generals had only recently defeated Huáscar's army at the Inca capital, Cuzco, and captured his brother to secure the throne. The disruption caused by the civil war had weakened the Inca Empire's cohesion. As in Cortés' conquest of the Aztecs, Pizarro was able to exploit the ill omens prophesied by the Inca priesthood, which had created misgivings among the Incas.

CHRONICLERS AND INFORMANTS

From the earliest explorations of Tierra Firme, chroniclers among the conquistadors left descriptions of the peoples they encountered. Later, historians in the 16th and 17th centuries wrote accounts of the Inca Empire and its past and descriptions of Inca culture and other peoples. Even so, the lack of a written language among any of the Andean Area civilizations before the Spanish conquest necessitates that these descriptions of Inca history and religion be complemented with archaeological, artistic and architectural images and evidence, particularly for pre-Inca cultures.

KNOT HISTORIES

Although no Andean culture developed a writing system, the recording device known as the *quipu*, a system of tied bundles of string with distinctive knotting and dyed colours, served as an *aide-mémoire* to designated *quipucamay-*

Below: Felipe Guaman Poma de Ayala travelling in Peru. He chronicled the conquest of the Inca Empire and Inca life and culture.

oqs (literally 'knot makers'). Many of the first records of Inca culture transcribed by Spanish priests were based on the memories of *quipucamayoqs* and their recitals of Inca accounts and records, religious concepts and beliefs, and history.

For example, in the 1560s and 1570s the Spaniard Sarmiento de Gamboa, who was given the task of recording Inca history by the fourth Viceroy of Peru, Francisco de Toledo, claimed to have interviewed more than 100 *quipucamayoqs*, 42 of whom he actually names.

Colleagues of the *quipucamayoqs* were the *amautas* – officially appointed court philosophers and historians. They were responsible for memorizing, recounting, interpreting, reinterpreting, amplifying, reciting and passing on to successors the legends and history, family trees and special events of the Inca kings and queens. They therefore became another principal source of Inca history, legend, religious belief and social organization, and in this way were invaluable not only to the early Spanish chroniclers but also to colonial officials struggling to implement Spanish administration and to collect produce and

Above: The quipu, *a device of knotted and dyed cotton and wool string, was used by special court officials to keep records.*

taxes. The *amautas'* detailed knowledge of the Inca *ayllu* (kinship), *mitamaes* (redistributed peoples) and *mit'a* (labour service) helped the Spaniards to take advantage of and adapt a system of obligations that was already in place.

INTERPRETING SOURCES

There was a danger, however, of taking such sources too literally, and of having to cope with the problems of conflicting accounts. Spanish chroniclers' and Catholic priests' transcriptions of the descriptions of Inca history and culture by *quipucamayoqs* and *amautas* were fraught with opportunities for misinterpretation. Deliberately or accidentally omitting some facts, embellishing others, and amending and reinterpreting what they had been told meant events could be retold to suit a particular bias. The resulting conflicting versions could be used to argue a particular legal claim or to justify a particular Spanish action or exploitative practice.

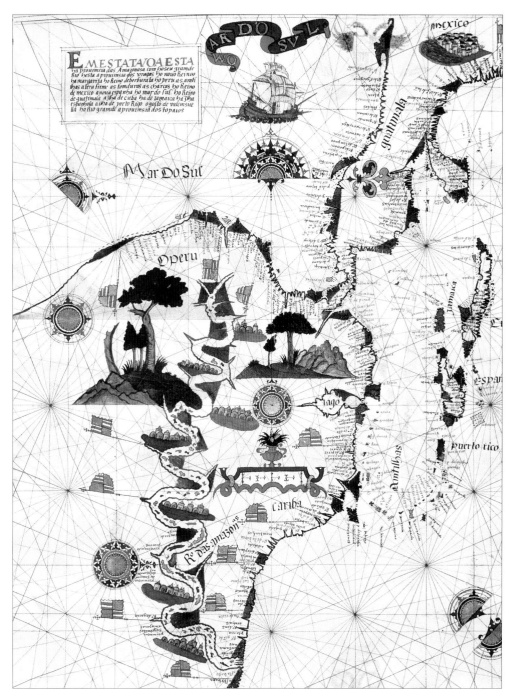

Nevertheless, the descriptions of Inca societies contained in these early records provide an invaluable source of information on Inca culture that can help make sense of archaeological evidence and vice versa.

SPANISH CHRONICLERS

About two dozen chroniclers' works provide information on the Incas and their contemporaries. Chief among them are the following writings. The mid-16th-century author Cieza de León's *Crónica del Peru* (1553 and 1554) contains much on Inca myth, while Juan de Betanzos' *Narrative of the Incas* (1557) recorded the subject from the point of view of the Inca nobility. Another record of Inca mythology is provided by Garcilasco de la Vega's (known as 'El Inca') *Comentarios Reales de los Incas* (1609–17), a comprehensive history of the Inca Empire.

The *Relación de los Quipucamayoqs* (written in Spain in 1608) comprises materials assembled to support the claims of a hopeful late pretender to the Inca throne, one Melchior Carlos Inca. He attempted to add depth and weight to his legitimacy by incorporating a version of the early foundation of Cuzco and the origin myth of the Incas, using as his source the manuscript of an inquest that had been held in 1542, the informants at which were four elderly *quipucamayoqs* who had served the Inca before the Spanish conquest.

Outside Cuzco, several sources provide accounts of myths from the regions of the empire. The exceptionally important Huarochirí manuscript, written in Quechua, *Dioses y Hombres de Huarochirí* (*c*.1610), records the myths of the central highlands of Peru. Two other sources relate accounts of the mythology of the peoples of the north Peruvian coast: Cabello de Balboa's *Miscelánea Antártica* (1586) and Antonio de la Calancha's *Crónica moralizada del Orden de San Augustínen el Perú* (1638).

THE CHRONICLERS

Accounts of mythology written by various Spanish-trained native Quechua-speaking authors include *Nueva Crónica y Buen Gobierno* by Felipe Guaman Poma de Ayala, written between 1583 and 1613, and *Relación de Antiguedades deste Reyno del Pirú*, which was written by Juan de Santacruz Yamqui Salcamaygua about 1613. Another set of documents, known as *idolatrías*, are records by Spanish priests and investigators who were attempting to stamp out idolatrous practices known to persist among the local populace under Spanish rule. These 17th-century documents are rich

Above: An early navigational map of the Spanish possessions in the Caribbean, New Spain, northern Peru and the Amazon.

in information on local myth based on interrogations of local authorities, native curers and 'witches' and other local diviners.

Lastly, the Jesuit priest Bernabé de Cobo, drawing principally from earlier chronicles, compiled the most balanced and comprehensive synthesis of Inca history and religion, in his monumental 20-year work *Historia del Nuevo Mundo*, books 13 and 14 of which, in particular, deal with Inca religion and customs.

LANGUAGES, DRAWINGS AND *QUIPU*

Hundreds of languages and dialects were spoken by the peoples throughout the Inca Empire, a fact even enshrined in Inca creation history. However, with no written language, the Incas relied on fine-line engraving and knot tying to keep records. Both these methods of recording data, events and customs provide modern scholars with valuable information with which to interpret the artefacts and structures from archaeological excavations. A combination of these finds and the information provided by the fine-line drawing and *quipus* enables us to discern the vast workings of the Inca Empire, and even pre-Inca times, and gives a greater understanding of Inca and other Andean cultures' beliefs about the universe.

QUECHUA, AYMARA, MOCHICA
The principal language of the Incas was Quechua (known to them as *Runa Simi*). This language was used throughout the empire for its administration and economic functions. Aymará, generally thought by linguists to be older than Quechua, was

Below: An Inca quipucamayoq *depicted by Guaman Poma de Ayala in his* Nueva Crónica y Buen Gobierno, c.1613.

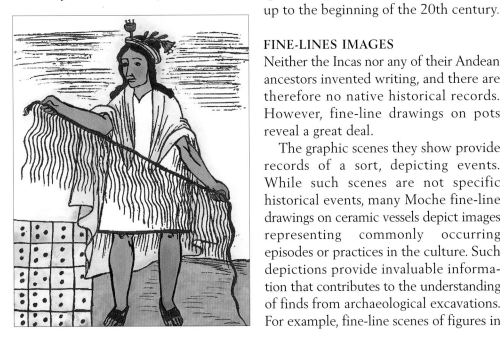

spoken throughout the highland region around the basin of Lake Titicaca. Some scholars group the two languages together under the name Quechuamaran. In northern coastal Peru, Mochica was spoken, the language of the ancient Moche, their ancestors and descendants. Both Quechua and Aymará are widely spoken today in the Central Andes by some six million or more people. Mochica continued to be spoken in part of northern coastal Peru up to the beginning of the 20th century.

FINE-LINES IMAGES
Neither the Incas nor any of their Andean ancestors invented writing, and there are therefore no native historical records. However, fine-line drawings on pots reveal a great deal.

The graphic scenes they show provide records of a sort, depicting events. While such scenes are not specific historical events, many Moche fine-line drawings on ceramic vessels depict images representing commonly occurring episodes or practices in the culture. Such depictions provide invaluable information that contributes to the understanding of finds from archaeological excavations. For example, fine-line scenes of figures in

Above: An Early Intermediate Period Moche pot with a 'narrative' scene, here showing weavers using backstrap looms.

burial rituals show deities, or priests-shamans in the roles of deities, which explains the presence of masks on the faces of the dead in Moche elite burials.

RECORDING WITH KNOTS
The *quipu* (or *khipu*; Quechua for 'knot') was a unique Inca Andean recording device. It comprised a central cord to which were attached numerous subsidiary cords or strings, like a fringe. The subsidiary cords were of different colours and they were tied into different sorts of knots with differing meanings. *Quipus* were mostly made of cotton cord, but llama wool was also sometimes used. About 700 *quipus* have been found.

ACCOUNTS OF MANY COLOURS
According to 16th- and 17th-century sources, prominent among which are the 16th-century conquistador and governor of Cuzco, Garcilaso de la Vega's *Comentarios Reales de los Incas* and the 17th-century *Historia et Rudimenta Linguae Piruanorum, quipus* had several uses.

Right: An Inca quipu, *which is unusually attached to a wooden rod. Specific* quipus *held records for individual cities.*

They were account 'books', in which the different colours, knots and sequences served as tallies of goods in Inca storehouses throughout the empire, or censuses of labour groups and sources; and they were mnemonic aids for recalling oral traditions – historical-literary events, including what modern scholars would call myth and legend.

The Incas used the decimal system in counting and knew positional mathematics. Knots in different positions on the same string and different types of knot were used to record thousands, hundreds and single units. The Incas were also aware of the concept of zero, duly represented by a cord without any knots. The key to reading such numerical *quipu* knots and positions was discovered in 1912 by Leland L. Locke. Analysing a *quipu* in the American Museum of Natural History, New York, he compared its knots and their positions to descriptions by Garcilaso de la Vega.

Additional meaning was recorded in the *quipu* through the use of colours and their sequences and combinations. Colours used included white, blue, yellow, red, black, green, grey, light brown and dark brown. Colours and their combinations represented types of goods or produce. For example, yellow could represent gold or maize corn.

SUBTLETIES OF MEANING

Further sophistication in meaning is represented by the orders of strings in series of the same colour. For example, in a counting of weapons stores, the most important ('noble') weapon was recorded at the left, and less noble weapons, in descending order, towards the right. The direction of the twisting of a cord itself added another layer of meaning: cords twisted to 'S' (clockwise) meant that the entire group referred to male categories or subject matter, while cords twisted to 'Z' (anti-clockwise) meant that the entire group referred to female categories or subject matter. Even individual knots can be made clockwise or anti-clockwise.

So-called 'literary' *quipus* incorporated textile ideograms (symbols used to represent whole words or concepts) among the strings. The same ideograms are found on Inca and pre-Inca textiles, pottery, sculpture and metalwork. The positions and numbers of knots below the ideograms indicate the syllables to be 'read'. The ideograms themselves relate to Inca (Andean) concepts of the universe, and to deities, man, animals and holy objects. An ideogram can also refer to a concept such as creation, the beginning of something, or to the elements and directions as represented by colours.

NAMING PLACES

The most recent breakthrough in *quipu* analysis has been made by Gary Urton and Carrie Brezine of Harvard University. Using a computer program designed to analyse the knot patterns in 21 *quipus* from a site in Puruchuco, an Inca administrative centre on the Peruvian coast, they discovered a recurring sequence of three figure-of-eight knots that appeared to represent a place name. The placement of this sequence at the start of these *quipus* represents the name for Puruchuco, and the patterns of colour combinations and string lengths appear to rank three levels of authority among them. Thus, wherever these *quipus* went, they could be identified with the Puruchuco administration and with Inca hierarchy, passing instructions down from high-level officials.

EXPLORERS AND ARCHAEOLOGISTS

The Spanish conquistadors peppered their chronicles with descriptions that gave glimpses of the Inca way of life. The accounts and histories of colonial officials and priests attempted to provide a complete record of Inca history, society and religion, even if biased consciously or unconsciously. In the 18th and 19th centuries, these publications began to be re-examined by European and American scholars. Excavations, crude for the most part, had begun to be undertaken in Europe and America by antiquarians curious to understand their own and other's pasts and eager to make collections of antiquities for museums.

TRAVELLERS' TALES

Although most such early 'archaeological' activity in the Americas took place in North America, some scholars and travellers began to realize that there were also

Above: Alexander von Humboldt made the first attempts to collect Inca and pre-Inca antiquities and to understand their sequence.

ruins and remnants of ancient structures and artefacts throughout what had been the Inca Empire and elsewhere in South America. Paramount among these was Alexander von Humboldt (1769–1859).

Von Humboldt was the epitome of the late 18th/early 19th-century natural historian. As a gentleman traveller, scholar and popular lecturer, his travels were a combination of exploration, adventure and a pursuit of new knowledge, as he sought to uncover the continent's natural history, geography, geology and ancient history. In his two landmark publications – *Political Essay on the Kingdom of New Spain* (1811) and *Researches Concerning the Institutions and Monuments of the Ancient Inhabitants of America* (1814) – and in popular lectures he attempted to accumulate and record systematically as much data about the Americas as he could and to present it in a detailed but succinct manner. He attempted to remain unbiased in the way he recorded the data, trying to keep recorded fact and description separate from interpretation and speculation. Nevertheless, he was at

Below: Alexander von Humboldt travelled throughout South America gathering information for his treatise on the continent.

Right: Alphons Stübel at the Gateway of the Sun, Middle Horizon Tiwanaku. He published his notes with Max Uhle in 1892.

the same time a pioneer in his attempts to explain the presence of humans in the New World and their manner of coming and spreading throughout the two continents, as well as the apparent independent rise of sophisticated civilizations whose ruins were plain to see. His work and lectures brought international recognition to the antiquities of South America.

Following von Humboldt's example, and no doubt inspired by the explorations of John L. Stephens and Frederick Catherwood in Mesoamerica, books listing and describing sites and types of artefacts were published from the 1850s, and attempts were made to establish a historical framework for the bewildering amount of material that was being rediscovered about the ancient ruins of Peru and Bolivia especially. Frances de Castelnau published his *Expédition dans les Parties Centrales de l'Amérique du Sud, Troisième Partie: Antiquités des Incas et Autre Peuples Anciens* in 1854; Johann Tschudi his

Below: Ceramic kero drinking vessels such as these were brought to private collectors and museums in the 18th and 19th centuries.

five-volume *Reisen durch Süd Amerika* in 1869; Charles Wiener his *Pérou et Bolivie* in 1874; Ephraim G. Squier, echoing Stephens and Catherwood, his *Peru: Incidents of Travel and Exploration in the Land of the Incas* in 1877; and E. W. Middendorf his three-volume *Peru* in 1893–5, all primarily descriptive works.

DESCRIPTION AND EXCAVATION

Books and papers by Sir Clements Markham in 1856–1910, especially *A History of Peru* (1892) and *The Incas of Peru* (1910), were early attempts to synthesize and explain the data. A few scholars went one step further and actually undertook excavations: Alphons Stübel and Wilhelm Reiss excavated the Ancon cemetery on the Peruvian coast, an ancient burial place near Lima, and published their results in *The Necropolis of Ancón in Peru* (1880–7). Adolph Bandelier carried out excavations of Tiwanaku sites on islands in the Titicaca Basin, the results of which were published in 1910, and of Tiwanaku itself in 1911.

Bridging the development of archaeology between these early classifications and descriptions of Andean materials stands the all-important figure of Max Uhle (1856–1944), who was inspired by Alphons Stübel. In 1892 he collaborated with him to publish *Die Ruinenstaette von Tiahuanaco*, a study based on notes and photographs taken by Stübel at Tiwanaku. From 1892 to 1912, Uhle carried out

regular fieldwork in Peru and Bolivia. Armed with a thorough knowledge of Inca and Tiwanaku pottery types, his excavations at Pachacamac on the Peruvian coast enabled him to establish the first breakthrough in the modern construction of the chronology of Andean ancient history. He knew Inca pottery to be 15th and 16th century in date; likewise he knew that Tiwanaku pottery was pre-Inca and completely unlike Inca ceramics. Therefore, he reasoned that the pottery he excavated at Pachacamac, because it was unlike Tiwanaku ware but was sometimes associated in layers with Inca ceramics at Pachacamac, must come between the two in date.

Uhle's work was the beginning of the assessment of series of styles of artefacts in combination with their relative position in the earth to build a chronology of the ancient cultures of the Andes. During the next 30 years he carried out other excavations, including work in Ecuador and northern Chile. He synthesized his own and others' work into a Peruvian area-wide chronology, the first for the Andean region, because he also linked his Ecuadorian and Chilean finds to the sequence. While many other scholars – European, North American and South American – worked throughout South America into the early 20th century, most of their work was limited to collecting, describing and classifying museum pieces.

MODERN INVESTIGATIONS

Modern methods in archaeology began in the 20th century. Alongside increasingly sophisticated reasoning to establish chronological sequences and relationships among artefacts and site structures, more careful methods of excavation and recording and numerous new scientific methods brought greater understanding – but also more questions. Archaeologists were no longer content just to describe, classify, date and display the past: they wanted to interpret and explain it too.

SEEKING ANSWERS TO QUESTIONS

Recording of stratigraphy (distinctive earth layers or associations between architectural features) enabled archaeologists to understand and interpret the relationships between artefacts, structures and other features. Archaeologists throughout the Americas began to direct their fieldwork towards finding evidence to answer special questions and understanding a much wider and deeper picture of ancient history. Investigations

Below: Late 20th-century excavations near the Coricancha in modern Cuzco revealed Inca foundations and water channels.

sought evidence on all aspects and classes of ancient society, not just on the elite and the exquisite.

In addition to excavations at the ruins of individual ancient cities, area surveys began to establish the extent of ancient remains, the relationships between them and the varying importance of different regions. Work focused on specific questions and historical problems: When did people first arrive in the Andes?

Above: The Black and White Portal at the Early Horizon temple at Chavín de Huántar. Early 20th-century archaeologists realized this was one of the first pre-Inca civilizations.

When was the first pottery made? When did agriculture begin? How great was the influence of different cultures, kingdoms and empires?

Excavations yielded increasing amounts of metalwork and textiles and evidence of the artefacts and methods used to make them. Studies went beyond describing and classifying the art on ancient Andean pottery and stonework and explained the meaning of their depiction of scenes and religious events.

MAKING DATES

During the first 60 years of the 20th century, Alfred L. Kroeber and John H. Rowe refined and expanded the timescale of Andean prehistory. On the basis of which materials were found and where they lay within the site's stratigraphy, Rowe defined a 'master sequence' of alternating Periods and Horizons that broadly defined the course of Andean ancient history. In the late 1940s the discovery of radiocarbon dating began to provide absolute dates for these cultural periods.

The first native Peruvian archaeologist, Julio C. Tello, began a life-long career excavating sites of the earliest periods of Andean civilization, notably Paracas cemetery on Peru's southern coast, Sechín Alto in northern Peru and Chavín de Huántar in the central Andes. He defined these remote periods when Andean civilization began and distinctive socio-economic and religious traits were established. In 1939, Tello and Kroeber established the Institute of Andean Research. Similarly, Luis E. Valcarcel, Tello's successor at the Lima Museo Nacional, promoted the rich interchange between different fields of study to clarify Inca and pre-Inca society.

INTERNATIONAL EXPEDITIONS

After World War Two, large-scale, long-running projects were undertaken throughout the Andes, addressing every period, from the earliest inhabitants to the Incas. Principal among these was the Virú Valley Project, begun in 1946 by Wendell C. Bennett, William D. Strong, James A. Ford, Clifford Evans, Gordon R. Willey, Junius Bird and Donald Collier.

In the 1960s and 1970s, Edward Lanning, Thomas Patterson and Michael Moseley worked on the central Peruvian coast. Thomas Lynch, Richard MacNeish and others clarified the Palaeoindian period. Seiichi Izumi and Toshihiko Sono of Tokyo University investigated Kotosh and other early ceramic ceremonial sites. Luis G. Lumbreras and Hernán Amat renewed the study of Chavín de Huántar, as did Richard L. Burger of the Peabody Museum. Donald Lathrap and his students worked in the eastern Andes and adjacent lowlands.

In the 1960s to 1980s, John Rowe, John Murra, Tom Zuidema, Gary Urton and many others renewed the study of the Incas, including excavations at Huánuco Pampa by Craig Morris and Donald Thompson. Large-scale projects were undertaken by Michael Moseley and Carol Mackay at Chan Chan, by William Isbell at Huari, by Christopher Donnan and Izumi Shimada in the Moche Valley and by Alan Kolata in the Tiwanaku Basin.

No summary of 20th-century Andean archaeology can ignore three of its most spectacular discoveries. In 1911 the young explorer Hiram Bingham rediscovered the Inca fortress and ceremonial precinct of Machu Picchu in the remote Urubamba Valley north of Cuzco, bringing it to world fame. In the 1980s, Walter Alva and Susana Meneses made astounding discoveries and excavations of fabulous, unlooted elite Moche tombs at Sipán in the Lambeyeque Valley of northern Peru. And in 1995 Johan Reinhard and Miguel Zárate discovered rich child

Left: John II. Rowe recording findings at the Inca palace of Huyna Capac, at Quisphuanca, Peru.

Above: Late 20th-century excavations by Walter Alva of the rare unlooted tomb of an Early Intermediate Period Moche lord at Sipán in the Lambayeque Valley, Peru.

burials high on Mt Ampato in the southern Andes, explaining the Inca ritual of *capacocha* sacrifice.

RETURN TO SOURCES

Alongside 20th- and 21st-century excavations and analyses, archaeologists still return to the original texts: the chronicles and records of the conquistadors and colonial officials. However biased or conflicting these may sometimes be, they remain the only first-hand accounts of Inca society. Uhle knew that the ruins of Tiwanaku were pre-Inca because the Incas themselves told the Spaniards that the city lay in ruins when they subjugated the area. Similarly, when Morris and Thompson discovered 497 stone structures arranged in orderly rows along the hillside south of Huánuco Pamapa, the stacked pottery vessels of agricultural produce revealed these buildings to be none other than examples of Inca provincial storehouses in which, as described in the chronicles, they collected the wealth of the empire for redistribution.

In this way, the first Spanish accounts continue to help explain excavation finds and to provide a basis for interpreting aspects of pre-Inca civilization, whose material remains often demonstrate a link with Inca practices and social functions.

TIMELINE: THE INCAS AND THEIR ANCESTORS

CHRONOLOGY OF ANDEAN AREA CIVILIZATION

The chronology of the Andean Area is complex. Archaeologists have developed a scheme based on technological achievements and on changing political organization through time, from the first arrival of humans in the area (15,000–3500BC) to the conquest of the Inca Empire by Francisco Pizarro in 1532. The pace of technological development varied in different regions within the Andean Area, especially during early periods in its history. The development of lasting and strong contact between regions, however,

Below: A wooden cup painted with an Inca warrior with shield and axe-spear.

spread both technology and ideas, and led to regions depending on each other to some degree. Sometimes this interdependence was due to large areas being under the control of one 'authority', while at other times the unifying link was religious or based on trade and technology.

The principal chronological scheme for the Andean Area comprises a sequence of eight time units: five Periods and three Horizons. Periods are defined as times when political unity across regions was less consolidated. Smaller areas were controlled by city-states, sometimes in loose groupings, perhaps sharing religious beliefs despite having different political organizations. The Horizons, by contrast, were times when much larger political units were formed. These units exercised political, economic and religious control over extended areas, usually including different types of terrain, rather than being confined to coastal valley groups or sierra city-states.

Different scholars give various dates for the beginnings and endings of the Periods and Horizons, and no two books on Andean civilization give exactly the same dates. The durations of Periods and

Above: The sacred Intihuatana (Hitching Post of the Sun) at Machu Picchu.

Horizons also vary from one region to another within the Andean Area, and charts increase in complexity as authors divide the Andean Area into coastal, sierra and Altiplano regions, or even into north, central and southern coastal regions and north, central and southern highland regions. The dates given here are a compilation from several sources, thus avoiding any anomalies among specific sources.

CHRONOLOGICAL PERIOD	DATES	PRINCIPAL CULTURES
Lithic / Archaic Period	15,000–3500BC	spread of peoples into the Andean Area hunter-gatherer cultures
Preceramic / Formative Period (Cotton Preceramic)	3500–1800BC	early agriculture and first ceremonial centres
Initial Period	1800–750BC	U-shaped ceremonial centres, platform mounds and sunken courts
Early Horizon	750–200BC	Chavín, Paracas, Pukará (Yaya-Mama) cults
Early Intermediate Period	200BC–AD600	Moche, Nazca and Titicaca Basin confederacies
Middle Horizon	AD600–1000	Wari and Tiwanaku empires
Late Intermediate Period	AD1000–1400	Chimú and Inca empires
Late Horizon	AD1400–1532	Inca Empire and Spanish Conquest

LITHIC / ARCHAIC PERIOD (40,000–3500BC)

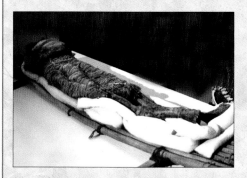

Above: This mummified body from the Chinchorros culture is 8,000 years old.

*c.*40,000 to *c.*20,000 years ago Ice-free corridors open up across the Bering Strait, but there is no evidence humans entered the New World until the late stages of this time period.

*c.*20,000BC Migrating hunter-gatherers, using stone-, bone-, wood- and shell-tool technologies, probably enter the New World from north-east Asia.

from *c.*15,000 years ago Palaeoindians migrate south and east to populate the Americas, reaching Monte Verde in southern Chile *c.*14,850 years ago.

*c.*8500–5000BC Hunter-gatherers occupy cave and rock shelter sites in the Andes (e.g. Pachamachay, Guitarrero, Tres Ventana and Toquepala caves). Evidence of tending of hemp-like fibre, medicinal plants, herbs and wild tubers.

*c.*5000BC First mummified burials in the Atacama Desert, Chinchorros culture.

Below: Mountains high in the Andes proved a challenge to early settlers.

PRECERAMIC / FORMATIVE PERIOD (3500–1800BC)

Above: Preceramic Period sculpture at the Temple of the Crossed Hands, Kotosh.

This period is sometimes also called the Cotton Preceramic.

*c.*3500–1800BC True plant domestication accomplished – cotton, squashes and gourds, beans, maize, potatoes, sweet potatoes, beans, chilli peppers. Llamas and other camelids herded on the Altiplano.

*c.*3000BC Coastal fishing villages such as Huaca Prieta flourish, using gourd containers but no ceramics, and produce early cotton textiles.

*c.*2800BC Early northern coastal civic-ceremonial centres begin at Aspero – Huaca de los Idolos and Huaca de los Sacrificios.

*c.*2400–2000BC Large, raised mound platforms are constructed at El Paraíso, La Galagada and Kotosh – Temple of the Crossed Hands. Spread of the Kotosh religious cult.

Below: Llamas and other camelids were first domesticated during this period.

INITIAL PERIOD (1800–750BC)

Above: View of the Colca Canyon shows terracing that began in this period.

Spread of pottery, irrigation agriculture, monumental architecture; religious processions and ritual decapitation begin.

from *c.*1800BC Sophisticated irrigation systems develop in coastal oases valleys, the highlands and Altiplano.

*c.*1800BC Construction at Moxeke includes colossal adobe heads.

*c.*1750BC Builders at La Florida bring the first pottery to this region.

*c.*1500BC Cerro Sechín flourishes.

*c.*1400–1200BC Sechín Alto becomes the largest U-shaped civic-ceremonial centre in the New World.

*c.*1300BC Construction of the five platform mounds at Cardál.

*c.*900BC U-shaped ceremonial complex at Chavín de Huántar begins.

Below: Garagay, central Peru, was a typical coastal U-shaped civic-ceremonial centre.

EARLY HORIZON (750–200BC)

Above: A stone severed head, with feline canines, from Chavín de Huántar.

Religious cults develop around Chavín de Huántar and Pukará. Decapitation, hallucinogenic drug use, spiritual transformation and ancestor worship become widespread.

from *c.*750BC The Old Temple at Chavín becomes established as a cult centre. Influence of the Lanzón deity and the Staff Deity spreads. The Paracas Peninsula serves as the necropolis site for several settlements, and the Oculate Being is shown on textiles and ceramics.

*c.*400–200BC The Old Temple at Chavín is enlarged to create the New Temple. The Chavín Cult spreads, especially at Kuntur Wasi and Karwa (Paracas).

*c.*400BC Rainfall fell in the Titicaca Basin. Pukará, northwest of the lake, is established, and becomes the centre of the Yaya-Mama cult.

*c.*200BC Chavín Cult influence waned.

Below: The Altiplano, south of the central Andes, was used for llama herding.

EARLY INTERMEDIATE PERIOD (200BC–AD600)

Above: The closely set stone blocks of the external walls of Sacsahuaman, Cusco.

The cohesion of Chavín disintegrates, and several regional chiefdoms develop in the coastal and mountain valleys.

from *c.*100BC Rise of the Nazca .

*c.*AD100 Burial of the Old Lord of Sipán in Lambayeque Valley.

*c.*AD100 to 500 The Nazca sacred ceremonial centre of Cahuachi flourishes.

*c.*1st century AD The Moche dynasty is founded in the northern coastal valleys.

*c.*AD250 Rise of oracle of Pachacamac.

*c.*AD300 Burial of the Lord of Sipán in Lambayeque Valley.

*c.*AD500 The Moche ceremonial platforms of the Huacas del Sol and de la Luna are the largest in the area.

*c.*AD700 Moche/Nazca power wanes.

Below: This giant Nazca desert geoglyph of the spider is visible from space.

MIDDLE HORIZON (AD600–1000)

Above: The Staff Deity depicted on the Gateway of the Sun at Tiwanaku.

Much of the Andean Area is unified in two empires: Tiwanaku in the south and Wari in the north. They share common beliefs around the creator god Viracocha.

*c.*AD300 Major construction of the central ceremonial plaza at Tiwanaku begins.

*c.*AD400–750 Major phases of building of elite residential quarters at Tiwanaku.

*c.*AD500 The rise of Huari, capital of the Wari Empire.

by *c.*AD600 Huari is a flourishing capital city and rival to Tiwanaku.

*c.*AD650 Pikillacta, the southernmost Wari city, is founded.

*c.*AD750–1000 Third major phase of palace building at Tiwanaku.

*c.*AD900–950 Burial of the Sicán Lords at Lambayeque.

Below: The reed boats on Lake Titicaca have been made for thousands of years.

LATE INTERMEDIATE PERIOD
(AD1000–1400)

Above: The Late Intermediate Period Sicán Tucume pyramid, Lambayeque Valley.

An era of political break up is characterized by new city-states, including Lambayeque, Chimú and Pachacamac, the Colla and Lupaka kingdoms, and numerous city-states in the central and southern Andean valleys.

*c.*AD1000 Tiwannaku and Wari empires wane as regional political rivalry reasserts itself.

*c.*AD1000 Wari city-state is abandoned.

*c.*AD1000 Chan Chan, the Chimú capital, is founded in the Moche valley.

*c.*1100 The Incas under Manco Capac, migrate into the Cuzco Valley, found Cuzco and establish the Inca dynasty.

*c.*1250 City of Tiwanaku abandoned, perhaps because of changes in climate.

*c.*1300 Sinchi Roca becomes the first emperor to use the title Sapa Inca.

Below: The city of Cuzco was founded by Manco Capac, its legendary first ruler.

LATE HORIZON
(AD1400–1532)

Above: The Inca hillside site of Winay Wayna overlooks the Urubamba River.

In just over 130 years the Incas build a huge empire and establish an imperial cult centred on Inti, the sun god, whose representative on earth is the Sapa Inca.

*c.*1425 Viracocha begins the Inca conquest of the Cuzco Valley.

1438 Pachacuti Inca Yupanqui defeats the Chancas to dominate the Cuzco Valley.

1438–71 Pachacuti begins the rebuilding of Cuzco as the imperial capital to the plan of a crouching puma.

1471 Fall of the Kingdom of Chimú.

1471–93 Inca Tupac Yupanqui expands the empire west and south, doubling its size.

1493–1526 Huayna Capac consolidates the empire, building fortresses, road systems, storage redistribution and religious precincts throughout the provinces.

Below: The Spaniards built S Domingo on the foundations of the Inca Coricancha.

Above: Manco Capac, legendary founder of the Inca dynasty and 'son of the sun'.

1526 Huayna Capac dies of smallpox without an agreed successor.

1526–32 Huayna Capac's son Huáscar seizes the throne but is challenged by his brother Atahualpa. A six-year civil war ends in the capture of Huáscar.

1530 Inca Empire at its greatest extent.

1532 Francisco Pizarro lands with a small army on the north coast and marches to meet Atahualpa at Cajamarca.

1532 Battle of Cajamarca and capture of Atahualpa, who is held for ransom.

1533 Atahualpa is executed.

1535 Francisco Pizarro founds Lima as his capital in Spanish Peru.

1541 Pizarro assassinated in his palace at Lima by Almagro and his associates.

Below: The sacred site of Machu Picchu was rediscovered by Hiram Bingham in 1911.

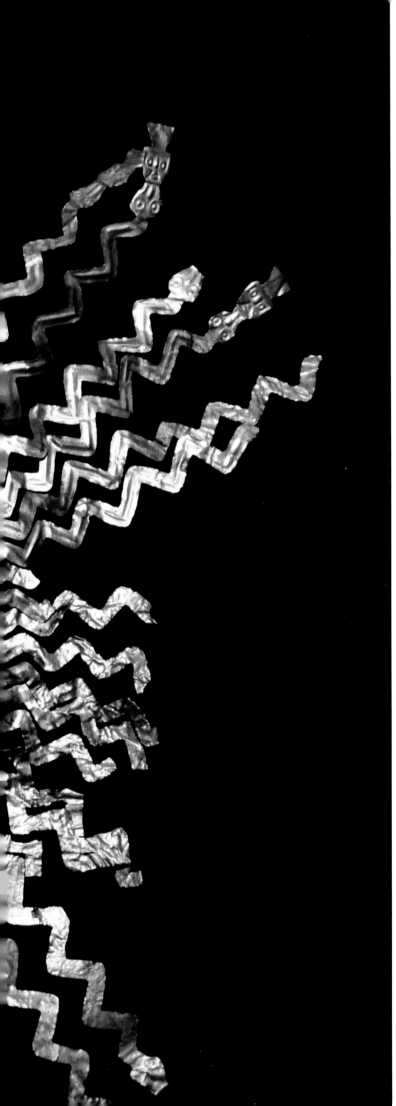

EMPIRE OF THE SUN

The Incas were a small group, or tribe, numbering perhaps 40,000 individuals or fewer in the Huantanay (Cuzco) Valley of modern central Peru. They were one group among many in the valley. Through conquest, first locally then beyond the valley, they built the largest empire that ever existed in the Americas. At its greatest extent, in AD1530, its northern border coincided roughly with the modern Ecuadorian–Colombian border, its southern extent stretched to modern central Chile, to the east it claimed regions into the lowlands bordering the Amazon Rainforest, and to the west it met the Pacific Ocean. Yet the Incas' rise to power lasted less than 100 years, and during the whole of this time they were engaged in wars of conquest or in the civil war at the end of this period.

Pachacuti Inca Yupanqui founded the imperial state of the Incas, and under his rule the Incas continued to dominate the Cuzco Valley. As the empire expanded, vast networks of roads were built to unite its far corners, coupled with impressive architectural and engineering feats that enabled planned towns and cities with great monuments to be built. Bridges were built and existing systems of terracing and irrigation expanded.

When the Spaniards under the leadership of Francisco Pizarro first arrived, the empire was still being expanded, but by the time of their third visit the empire was split by civil war. This war led eventually to the death of two rival sons of the Inca ruler, Huayna Capac, and the victory of Pizarro.

Left: The skilled metallurgists of the La Tolita culture were among many to depict the sun as a rayed golden mask.

LAND OF THE FOUR QUARTERS

The Incas called their world Tahuantin-suyu (or Tawantinsyu), literally meaning 'the land of the four united quarters'. Cuzco, the capital city, formed the focal point (although it was not the geographical centre) on which the four quarters were oriented and from which they emanated.

To the north-east of Cuzco was Antisuyu, the smallest quarter and the only one that did not border on the Pacific Ocean. To the north-west, stretching to the northernmost borders of the empire, was Chinchaysuyu. This quarter's northern extent had, in fact, only recently been extended into Quito province by the last conquering Sapa Inca, Huayna Capac (1493–1526), shortly before the arrival of the conquistador Francisco Pizarro in 1531. South and west of Cuzco was Cuntisuyu, second in size, and to the south-east was the largest of the four quarters, Collasuyu.

Below: Ephraim George Squier was the first to show a detailed plan of Inca Cuzco as a puma, its head formed by the fortress-temple of Sacsahuaman and its body and tail by the streets and water channels.

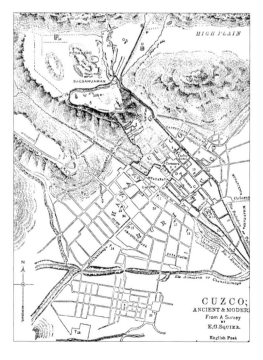

Above: The Huacaypata Plaza, Cuzco, now the Plaza de Armas, was the site of ritual celebrations at solstices and festivals.

UNEQUAL QUARTERS

The four quarters were not only unequal in size but in population. They also differed extensively in the types of terrain they encompassed. Together they comprised a vast territory stretching from modern Ecuador to central Chile, north to south, and from the Pacific coast to the eastern flank of the Andes mountain chain, west to east. The empire was inhabited by a great variety of peoples and languages, each with long traditions of local development, masterfully united and socially co-ordinated and manipulated by their Inca masters. The Incas recognized this diversity as the deliberate actions of the creator god Viracocha, who, having formed the second world and its human inhabitants out of clay, dispersed them after giving them the clothing, skills and languages of the different tribes and nations.

Mention of the partition of the empire into four quarters was, as such, virtually ignored in most of Inca history. One legend, however, recounted in Garcilaso de la Vega's early 17th-century work, *Commentarios Reales de los Incas*, describes the division as the work of an 'Un-named Man' who appeared at Tiwanaku after the destruction of a previous world by great floods. This near lack of explanation is especially curious given the emphasis in Inca legendary history on the progress of the state creation from Lake Titicaca – near the geographical centre of the empire – towards the north and west, into the Huantanay (Cuzco) Valley.

This progress in one direction makes sense for Antisuyu, Chinchaysuyu and Cuntisuyu, but not for Collasuyu, which lies almost entirely to the south of Lake Titicaca. One explanation might lie in the fact that the Incas recast the origin mythology of the peoples of Collasuyu in order to bolster their own claims of origin from the Titicaca Basin, thus legitimizing their right to rule the region. The Incas were aware of the remains of Tiwanaku to the south and west of the lake, and no doubt of the relics of other previous great cities of the region, and must have recognized them as the centres

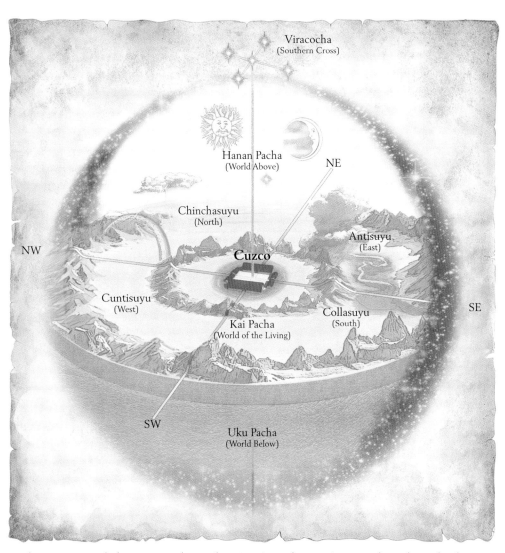

Right: A diagram of the land of the four quarters, based on a 1613 sketch by Juan de Santa Cruz Pachacuti Ymaqui Salcamaygua.

of former power bases. The Incas explained to the Spaniards that Tiwanaku lay in ruins when they invaded and conquered the Titicaca Basin.

THE FOUNDING OF CUZCO

The Incas regarded their capital at Cuzco as being at the centre of the world. Once again, Inca legendary history and heavenly associations formed the basis of their arrangments, for Cuzco equally reflected state and celestial organization. According to legend, Pachacuti Inca rebuilt the imperial city and the Coricancha (Sun Temple) in stone, being inspired by the ruined stone masonry of Tiwanaku. Indeed, archaeological excavations in the capital have shown that the Incas had no tradition of megalithic stone masonry before about AD1350–75, according to radiocarbon dating. The city was divided into upper (*hanan*) and lower (*hurin*) sections, respectively the quarters of the two social divisions of the populace believed to have been ordered by the first ruler, Manco Capac. Again according to legend,

Pachacuti named the renewed city 'lion's body' (by which the Spanish chronicler meant a puma), and, from above, the plan of the city indeed resembles a crouching puma with a head and tail.

HIGHWAYS AND LINES

From the central plaza, Huacaypata, four great imperial highways and four sacred cosmic lines radiated to the four quarters. From the nearby Coricancha emanated 41 sacred *ceque* lines: sightings lines to the horizons and beyond. They were grouped into upper and lower sets and further divided into four quarters. The upper set was associated with Hanan Cuzco and with the quarters of Antisuyu (north-east) and Chinchasuyu (north-west), while the lower set was associated with Hurin Cuzco and with the quarters of Collasuyu (south-east) and Cuntisuyu

Left: Inca surveyors linked the provinces of the entire empire with a masterly engineered road system.

(south-west). Together these highways, cosmic lines and *ceques* integrated the capital and the four quarters into the Inca state religion focused on Inti, the sun god, as a near equal to the creator Viracocha – perhaps another reason why they did not emphasize the history of the divisions.

ROADMAP OF THE STARS

A link with the heavens was further enhanced by the association of each of the four great highways along a route approximating (except when having to to go around hills and mountains) a north–south/east–west axis of Mayu (literally 'celestial river'), commonly known as the Milky Way. In the course of 24 hours, ancient Andeans observed that Mayu crosses its zenith in the sky, and in so doing forms two intersecting axes oriented north-east/south-west and south-east/north-west. Thus, the divisions of the sky provided a celestial grid against which their world of Tahuantinsuyu was projected.

CUZCO AND BEYOND

The Inca Empire stretched more than 4,200km (2,600 miles) from north to south and east to west across the Andes, from the Amazon rainforests and Argentine plains to the Pacific coast. Throughout this vast area lived a variety of peoples whose earlier cultural evolution united them locally and regionally, especially at an economic and religious level. This was exploited by the Incas, who imposed imperial rule and economic stability on the empire.

ALL ROADS LEAD TO CUZCO

Imperial Cuzco, the capital city, was considered to be the navel of the Inca world. From it and to it led all roads, both physically and spiritually. This network linked peoples and cultures as varied as fishing communities, such as the Uru in the Lake Titicaca Basin, and the Kingdom of Chimú on the Peruvian north coast, a state whose sophistication might have rivalled the Incas. The empire reached its greatest extent beyond the Cuzco Valley in less than 100 years of conquests.

Below: Tambo Colorado, at the end of a major road running west, was one of many planned provincial administrative capitals.

SPREADING CIVILIZATION

A number of distinctive Inca cultural traits have been identified, which they spread to greater and lesser extents throughout the empire. These include: a corporate style of architecture, settlement planning, artefact styles, large-scale engineering works and terracing.

In the Cuzco area, most residential buildings (*kanchas*) were rectangular, single-room and single-storey affairs, arranged around courtyards. They were made of fieldstones or adobe bricks,

Above: The vast Altiplano of Collasuyu, Bolivia, south of Cuzco, was added to the empire through the conquests of Sapa Inca Tupac Yupanqui (1471–93).

gabled, with thatched roofs, and had doors, windows and internal niches usually of trapezoidal shape. A second basic form, the *kalanka*, was a rectangular hall used for several public functions. Structures for state purposes were mostly, but not always, made of finely cut and fitted stone. Most were in the capital and its immediate environs; fitted-stone architecture was rare in the provinces and restricted to special state buildings.

In settlement planning, the Incas practised a policy of relocating peoples away from their homelands for political and economic reasons. In such settlements, Inca engineers laid out *kancha* enclosures in blocks around Inca-style state administrative buildings where needed. Some provincial Inca settlements were established for specific purposes, perhaps one of the best known being Huánuco Pampa, an Inca imperial city about 675km (420 miles) north-west of Cuzco in the Chinchaysuyu quarter, which was established as a seat of provincial administration and also for the storage and redistribution of the products of the empire.

Above: Huánuco Pampa, a provincial administrative capital in Chinchasuyu, lay on the main northern trunk road up the spine of the empire, heading all the way to Quito.

In some provincial settlements, the Incas relied on local technology and adapted themselves to local political and social organization while retaining an over-arching control. In such cases any evidence of Inca presence, conquest and rule is found more in material culture, particularly pottery (but also textiles and metalwork), of distinctive Inca decorative design and techniques.

The vast majority of settlements were not Inca in origin and were, apart from the relocated populations in Inca-planned towns, left in their native styles and plans. Again, Huánuco Pampa provides an important example: the surrounding villages retained their local native character and Inca rule was exerted indirectly through local leaders.

Throughout the empire, Inca engineers were famous for their works. There were roads, bridges, agricultural terracing and accompanying systems of irrigation canals. Imperial highways linked Cuzco with the provincial capitals. Major imperial highways went north-west to Vilcashuaman, Huánuco Pampa, Cajamarca, Tumibamba

and Quito and south-east to Chucuito, Paria, Tupiza, La Paya, Santiago and other cities. Westward-running highways branched off to major coastal cities – Tumbes, Pachacamac, Tambo Colorado, Nazca and others – and a parallel highway ran along the Peruvian coast as far as Atico. In many cases pre-existing roads were incorporated and it is often difficult to identify roads as specifically Inca-made unless there is also associated Inca architecture, or sometimes evidence of inhabitants. Similarly with bridges: it is often only the presence of stone foundations and Inca artefacts at river crossings that indicates where an Inca bridge stood.

Land terracing, especially throughout the Andes, was constructed to take advantage of every available opportunity to extend land for growing, especially maize. Again, it is not always possible to identify specifically Inca terracing from pre-Inca work without other associated Inca features, but it is certain that with the expansion of Inca domination the extent of terracing increased greatly.

KINSHIP AND TAXES

The Incas exploited and perhaps consolidated the economic and social arrangement called *ayllu*. This was a kinship charter based on actual or imagined descent

between groups working the different environments between highlands and lowlands, especially farming and llama herding. Such a group of related people was an organization for both labour exchange and a common ownership of property, possessions and rights; it also established, monitored and regulated rules of social conduct, and solved social problems at various levels. In other words, it incorporated rights and responsibilities.

The Incas employed a state tax system of agricultural produce divided into three categories; land was divided accordingly to support each category. The first was for the support of the gods – in practical terms it went to the priests, other religious functionaries and shrine attendants. The second went to the emperor, to support the imperial household and into storage for redistribution in times of need. The third was for the communities themselves; it was collected, stored and distributed annually by local officials.

In addition to taxation there was a labour tax, or obligation, called *mit'a*. This was an annual draft of able-bodied males to undertake public work.

Although both *ayllu* and *mit'a* were established in pre-Inca times throughout much of the Andes, the Incas exploited and used them more extensively.

BUILDING AN EMPIRE

The Inca Empire began and ended in conflict. Its downfall was hastened by the Spanish invasion, yet, when the Spaniards arrived, the Incas were themselves engaged in civil war.

THE CUZCO VALLEY

The founding of the empire is obscured in elaborate legend and myth invented by the Incas. It began with a legendary figure and first ruler, Manco Capac, leader of the *ayars*, the legendary ancestors, and founder of the Inca dynasty. The founding involved mystical birth from the earth, the designation of Inca superiority and their destiny to rule.

There were four brothers, of whom Manco was senior, and four sisters/wives – providing consistency with the division of the empire into four quarters. It was Manco who ordered the division of the people into the *hurin* and *hanan* – the upper and the lower – and who formed 'the allies' into ten lineage groups: the ten *ayllus* of commoners at Cuzco to complement the ten royal *ayllus* of his and his brothers' descendants. After migration from Lake Titicaca and many

adventures, Manco, his sister/wife, and other sisters, and their son Sinchi Roca arrived in the Valley of Cuzco, where Manco organized the building of the city. Sinchi Roca duly inherited the throne and allegedly commanded the people of the valley to cultivate potatoes. He was followed by his son Lloque Yupanqui. We have no idea how long these rulers reigned, or if there were more than are named.

Archaeology provides only hints of the development of Inca power in the Cuzco Valley. We know little of what lies buried beneath modern Cuzco, and almost nothing of what lies beneath the 16th-century Inca city. It has been occupied continuously since Inca times, if not before, and many Inca structures were themselves used as foundations for Spanish colonial and later structures.

DEVELOPING POWER

Ceramic styles show us that the Incas were probably a local tribe, one of several in the valley, and that Cuzco began to emerge as a regional centre in the Late Intermediate Period from the early 13th

Above: Manco Capac allegedly founded Inca Cuzco and ruled in the 12th century, in the Late Intermediate Period.

century. No individual buildings, or any distinctive architectural style, can be identified with the Incas or with a specific Inca ruler until the reign of Pachacuti Inca Yupanqui (1438–71). We do not know whether the Incas ruled Cuzco from this early time, coexisted with their neighbours or actually lived elsewhere.

What is certain, however, is that they began to dominate the valley from at least about the beginning of the 15th century. A sort of defined style began to emerge in the late 14th and early 15th centuries and was strengthened by Pachacuti Inca Yupanqui. It was he who began the formation of the Inca imperial state; and the Late Horizon, which began c.1400, is defined by the beginning of his hegemony.

The intervening rulers between Lloque Yupanqui and Pachacuti are a mere name list: Mayta Capac, Capac Yupanqui, Inca

Left: Puca Pukara fort near Cuzco was used in wars against the neighbouring peoples in the Cuzco Valley and adjacent valleys.

Roca, Yahuar Huacac, Viracocha Inca and Inca Urco. We have little knowledge of their achievements other than that they inherited rulership of the Cuzco Valley, and continued to dominate their neighbours and strengthen their power within the valley. Mayta Capac defeated a local tribe called the Alcaviçças, who were apparently dissatisfied with the Inca overlordship in the valley.

WAR AGAINST THE CHANCAS

Only Viracohca Inca and Urco emerge from legend as real people. During troubled times, undoubtedly the war with the Chancas (another valley tribe), Viracocha claimed that the god Viracocha came to him in a dream, calmed his fears and inspired him to rule. However, he and his son and named heir, Urco, fled Cuzco with much of the populace when the Chancas advanced on the city. Urco enjoyed the shortest reign – less than a year in 1438 – if he actually reigned at all.

Below: The tiered wall of Sacsahuaman, which forms the north-west quarter (Chinchasuyu) of Inca Cuzco.

His brother, Yupanqui, was more steadfast and stayed to defend the city. He too claimed divine inspiration, in an earlier incident giving him a vision of the future. In official Inca history, Yupanqui rallied his companions and repulsed the first two attacks. He called upon the gods for help and the very stones in the field allegedly became Inca warriors. The Chancas were defeated and, taking the name Pachacuti Inca ('Earth-shaker King'), he assumed the throne.

TO THE LIMITS OF THE EMPIRE

The date of 1438, which comes from the chronicler Miguel Cabello de Valboa, marked Pachacuti's defeat of the Chancas and his succession to the throne. He subdued the Cuzco Valley and declared all Quechua-speakers there to be honorary Inca citizens. He began Inca imperial aspirations by conquering the Lupaqa, Colla and other city-states to the south-east around Lake Titicaca. Then he turned his armies over to his son and chosen heir, Tupac Inca Yupanqui, to continue campaigning, while he returned to Cuzco and devoted his energies to consolidating the power of the Incas.

Above: Pachacuti Inca Yupanqui expanded the Inca Empire with conquests into Cuntisuyu, Chinchasuyu and Collasuyu.

Pachacuti is credited with developing Inca statecraft and with organizing the institutions and systems that were the hallmarks of Inca rule: national taxation and labour levies, roadways and an imperial communication network, and extensive warehousing of food and other commodities for redistribution throughout the empire. He also established the official Inca state religion based on worship of Inti – the sun – and commissioned much building in the city, including the temple-fortress of Sacsahuaman, which was dedicated to the worship of Inti.

Tupac (1471–93) extended the empire to its greatest extent with conquests to the north and south, especially of the powerful Chimú Kingdom on the north coast, defeating King Minchançaman. His successor, Huayna Capac (1493–1526), campaigned throughout the empire, largely consolidating earlier gains. He had recently subjugated the kingdom of Quito when he died suddenly of smallpox. In the turmoil that followed, two of his sons, half-brothers by different wives, claimed the succession: Huáscar, governor of Cuzco, and Atahualpa, who controlled the army in the north.

CIVIL WAR

Spanish sources leave some doubt as to whether Huayna Capac, the twelfth Inca ruler, had actually named his successor when he died suddenly. Some sources say there was an heir apparent, a young son Ninancuyuchi, others that Huayna Capac favoured his son Huáscar, or that he secretly hoped that another son, Atahualpa, would use his control of the army to supplant Huáscar. Still other sources indicate that he had planned to divide the empire among several sons, or even that the empire was so far extended that it was effectively dividing itself in 1526.

Needless to say, the various factions that still existed at the time of the Spanish conquest recited to Spanish chroniclers the versions of events and descendants that suited them. Nevertheless, upon Huayna Capac's death, the Spaniards had just arrived off the northern coast of the empire and the Incas plunged into a bloody civil war that itself threatened the demise of the empire and all it stood for.

Below: Soldiers of Atahualpa's army lead his brother Huáscar into captivity after his defeat at the Battle of Huánuco Pampa.

ONE THRONE: THREE HEIRS?
Huayna Capac had campaigned in the north of the empire for ten years. He had gone north, originally to quell a rebellion in Quito province, taking with him his sons Ninancuyuchi and Atahualpa. In Cuzco he left four governors, one of whom was Huáscar, another of his sons by his many wives. When an epidemic of smallpox broke out in the north and

Above: An Inca soldier painted on a wooden kero *drinking vessel, wearing traditional battle dress – a tunic and feather headdress.*

Huayna Capac contracted it, he anointed in formal ceremony his son Ninancuyuchi as his heir. But Ninancuyuchi also died of smallpox, and this situation left a dilemma and a plethora of possible claimants to the throne.

Huáscar seized the throne in Cuzco but was contested by Atahualpa, his younger half-brother. Atahualpa had been involved in the campaign against and subjugation of the Quito region in the far north of the empire. At his father's death he was left in command of the Inca armies of the north. At the death of Huayna Capac and Ninancuyuchi, he at first seemed to accept Huáscar's rise to power and ordered new palaces to be built for Huáscar in the northern city of Tumipampa. The local chief, Ullco Colla, however, resented Atahualpa and spread rumours of a plot against Huáscar. In the ensuing intrigue, Atahualpa and Huáscar became enemies and the former marched to confront his brother. The Inca court split into two supporting factions and civil war raged for six years.

BATTLE BETWEEN BROTHERS
Huáscar declared Atahualpa to be *auca* – a treasonous enemy of the state. He sent the army he commanded in Cuzco to attack Atahualpa and capture him in Quito.

Below: The imposing tiered walls of Sacsahuaman imply its use as a fortress as well as its main purpose as a temple to Inti.

But in a major battle Huáscar's forces were utterly defeated, and Atahualpa continued a relentless march south.

Huáscar sent larger armies against him. There were running battles and Huascar's forces were defeated but without conclusive results. Rivalry even broke out among Huáscar's generals. Huáscar sent even greater forces against Atahualpa, who again defeated them, until finally, in 1532, Huáscar himself marched with an army against him. Atahualpa's experience in the northern campaigns finally proved decisive, and this time Huáscar was taken prisoner. The final battle took place at Huánuco Pampa, north-west of Cuzco.

Atahualpa, whose forces were flushed with their victories, relied on speed. His generals marched immediately against Huáscar before further reinforcements could arrive from Cuzco. Given what had already transpired, Atahualpa offered no peace negotiations. The battle apparently lasted most of the day until Huáscar's troops broke and Huáscar was forced to flee with his immediate retinue of about 1,000 retainers and troops. Atahualpa's forces soon overtook him, however, seized Huáscar and put the remainder of his followers to death.

Above: Dressed in distinctive tunics and armed with axe-headed spears and shields, Inca armies subdued the empire.

ROYAL SACRILEGE
The ruthlessness of this prolonged war continued when Atahualpa marched on and captured Cuzco. He feigned a plan to return Huáscar to the throne as Sapa Inca and declared a day for the event. He commanded the attendance of the nobles and leaders of the empire, the provincial governors and chief administrators, many of whom were related to Huáscar, indeed to Atahualpa as well. Together they comprised the *panaca*, descendants of the royal household.

The provinces of the empire had been divided since the civil war had begun. Many cities had simply continued life as usual, while others in the most remote or recently conquered reaches of the empire rebelled or simply ignored Inca rule for the time being, awaiting the outcome of events. Now that Atahualpa was victorious, and apparently in control, however, they were being called upon to declare their loyalty.

Once everyone was gathered in Cuzco, Atahualpa had them all slain, so effectively ending further resistance by destroying the *panaca's* very existence.

Yet Atahualpa went further still in his aim to eliminate the royal family: he ordered the burning of the mummy of Tupac Yupanqui, the tenth Sapa Inca and ancestor of the *panaca*.

CONQUEST OF THE EMPIRE

Even before Francisco Pizarro (1475–1541) began his Andean explorations, an entire empire, that of the Aztecs, had been conquered in Mesoamerica by his countryman Hernán Cortés.

PIZARRO'S RETURN

A veteran of an expedition to Panama in 1509, Pizarro was eager to emulate Cortés. After two voyages from Panama to the South American mainland, he had returned with enough knowledge of the coast, stories of rich cities inland and to the south, and examples of gold and silver objects and textiles to convince him another civilization of great wealth lay to the south.

In 1526, had he attempted on his second expedition to invade the fringe of the Inca Empire, he would surely have been defeated. The empire was at its height under Sapa Inca Huayna Capac (1493–1526), with provincial garrisons and a strong army able to move quickly from centre to province along an efficient road system. In 1531, however, an attack

Below: The walls and defensive gateway of the fortress city of Rumicolca, about 35km (21 miles) southeast of Cuzco.

and pillaging of the coastal, provincial port of Tumbes by the inhabitants of Puná Island went unavenged, for Capac's successor, Huáscar, was otherwise engaged.

Pizarro visited Tumbes in 1526. When he returned in 1532, he still had the two native interpreters from the town, whom he had taken with him to Spain to raise royal permission and funds for his third expedition. Now the Inca Empire was in a state of turmoil. Huáscar's army had recently been defeated by his half-brother, Atahualpa, Huáscar had been captured, and Atahualpa had seized the throne.

IMPERIAL OMENS

Even before this civil war, Huayna Capac told his sons that Inti, the sun god, had informed him that his reign was the last of the twelve Sapas. Inca rule would end with the arrival of powerful strangers, whom he believed to be the foreigners recently reported arriving by sea on the north coast. Their coming was foretold by ill omens: during ceremonies honouring Inti, an eagle was mobbed and killed by buzzards and the priests prophesied disaster; and one night the new moon had three halos – one red, one black, one smoky.

Above: Francisco Pizarro, who was born illegitimate in Trujillo, Estremadura, turned from swineherd into soldier of fortune.

The priests said the red ring foretold war between the Sapa's descendants, the black ring the demise of Inti and the smoke the vanishing of the empire. These were weaknesses that Pizarro could exploit.

Huayna Capac ordered his sons to obey the strangers, for they were in every way superior. Written after the fact, the Spanish-Inca historian Garcilaso de la Vega's account appears to be a combination of political expediency and rationalization for the collapse of the empire, which the Incas believed to be perfect. In reality, weaknesses in the Inca hierarchy, civil war, the size of the empire and the shear audacity of Pizarro better explain the subsequent events.

THE MARCH TO CAJAMARCA

The arrival of reinforcements from Panama brought Pizarro's grand army to 260 men (198 foot soldiers and 62 cavalry). Tumbes had supported Huáscar in the civil war, providing a ready-made ally. Leaving a garrison in Tumbes, Pizarro marched inland with his best troops.

Left: A fanciful depiction of Atahualpa before his capture by Pizarro. Inca soldiers did not march and fight naked.

20 cavalrymen, then Hernando Pizarro with another 20, were sent to seek Atahualpa, who waited for them at his quarters, together with his court and some 400 warriors.

The Spaniards had to push their way through the Inca ranks. Accounts of the exchange vary: de Soto impressed the Incas with a display of horsemanship, then invited Atahualpa to the Spanish camp. Hernando arrived. Atahualpa declared that he was fasting and would visit on the next day. He claimed that one of his chiefs had killed three Spaniards and a horse back on the march. Hernando denied that any Inca could overcome a Spaniard. Atahualpa complained that one of his provincial chiefs had disobeyed him and Hernando bragged that ten horsemen could put down the revolt. *Chicha* was brought in large gold vessels. Etiquette was served; macho was displayed. It was left at that.

Below: Hernando Pizarro and Hernando de Soto were sent by Francisco Pizarro as envoys to Atahualpa at Cajamarca.

To win more allies, he adopted a pacific approach. He forbade looting, and encouraged his Dominican friars to convert the heathens; but opposition, where met, was put down brutally – opposing provincial chiefs were burned as examples. His campaign became a crusade.

Atahualpa marched his army – reportedly 40–50,000 warriors – nearly 1,600km (1,000 miles) to Cajamarca to await Pizarro, who was himself travelling on a litter. With 110 foot soldiers and 67 cavalrymen, Pizarro camped near Tambo Grande and sent his lieutenant, Hernando de Soto, to reconnoitre. De Soto returned with an Inca official bearing gifts and an invitation to Cajamarca. Pizarro accepted the gifts, sent the official back with gifts of his own and a message that he represented the most powerful emperor in the world, offering service against the Sapa's enemies, and continued his slow march south and east towards the 4,000m (13,000ft) pass to Cajamarca.

Atahualpa sent a gift of ten llamas. The messenger gave an account of the war with Huáscar, and Pizarro allegedly delivered a speech declaring peaceful intentions, but was prepared for war if challenged. Another day's march involved being greeted by an Inca official with *chicha* (maize liquor) in gold cups – he was to lead the Spaniards to Cajamarca.

An allied chief whom Pizarro had sent to Atahualpa returned. He attacked Atahualpa's official, calling him a liar, and claimed that the Sapa had refused to receive him. He said that Cajamarca was deserted and Atahualpa had deployed his army on the plain ready for war. Atahualpa's ambassador retorted that Cajamarca had been vacated to make it ready for Pizarro – that it was the Sapa's custom to camp with this army on campaign (meaning the civil war). These exchanges must have left Pizarro more confused than ever.

Finally Pizarro, his men suffering from altitude sickness and exhaustion, climbed the hills into Cajamarca Valley. At any time Atahualpa could have destroyed him, yet he did nothing.

ETIQUETTE OBSERVED

Pizarro marched into Cajamarca's main courtyard on 15 November 1532, passing the vastly larger Inca army, his men arranged in three divisions to make the most of his comparatively meagre force. No envoy awaited or arrived. De Soto and

CAPTURE AND REGICIDE

Atahualpa arrived at the Spanish camp late on 16 November. There had been debate among his advisers and he had decided to visit with an armed entourage. Inca warriors lined the route and surrounding grasslands. Atahualpa, carried by his chiefs on a litter adorned with gold and silver plates, was preceded by elite warriors in colourful chequered livery, singing, dancing and sweeping the roadway before him. Atahualpa himself was bedecked with gold and turquoise jewellery, and the entire retinue displayed his wealth and majesty.

The journey was less than 6km (4 miles), yet Atahualpa hesitated, sent a messenger that he would come the next day, then changed his mind and resumed progress, now with only 6,000 unarmed followers. Atahualpa's indecision revealed a lack of human confidence despite his obsession with displaying his dignity and status as a living god. He simply could not understand the nature of the men he was dealing with.

SLAUGHTER AND CAPTURE
Entering the empty courtyard, Atahualpa was greeted by Pizarro's friar, Valverde, brandishing a Bible and a crucifix. He delivered a discourse on Christianity.

Left: In early meetings with Atahualpa's noble ambassadors, Francisco Pizarro and Hernando De Soto professed peace.

Historians will forever remain unsure of the ensuing events. Despite the message having to pass through an interpreter, it seems clear that Atahualpa understood what was being demanded of him: renunciation of everything he believed in, of his entire world. Allegedly, Valverde handed him the Bible; allegedly he threw it down, pointing at the sun and declaring 'My God still lives.'

Valverde retrieved the Bible and retreated. Pizarro gave the signal to attack: a cannon was fired into the crowd, followed by arquebuses (long-barrelled guns); then his men charged. Atahualpa's chiefs fought with bare hands to save their emperor, and were butchered in the attempt. A wall collapsed in the frenzy of retreating natives. Those trapped in the courtyard were slaughtered until night fell and Atahualpa was taken captive. Thus treachery was accomplished. It must have seemed to Pizarro that this was the only way to succeed against clearly overwhelming odds. The chronicler Zárete records that the whole plot had been discussed and decided the night before. Pizarro had indeed emulated Cortés by taking the emperor hostage.

GREED AND BETRAYAL
The passivity of Atahualpa's people and army is astounding. They simply melted away, leaving their possessions in camp. The Spaniards looted Cajamarca and the chiefs' tents, seized the army's llama herds and raped the women abandoned in the royal baths.

The remainder of the story is equally sordid. Realizing Pizarro's lust for gold and silver, Atahualpa offered to fill the 5.5 by 7m (18 by 23ft) room in which he was held, as high as he could reach, with gold. Pizarro demanded that, in addition, the adjoining smaller room be filled twice

Above: Having captured Atahualpa at Cajamarca, Pizarro imprisoned him in a palace room while a ransom was negotiated.

with silver. Atahualpa agreed to these demands, asked for two months, and ordered the collection of gold and silver objects from all over the empire.

At Atahualpa's request, three Spaniards, including de Soto, were sent to Cuzco to hasten the collections. They found the captive Huáscar, who offered to treble his half-brother's ransom. Learning this, Atahualpa gave secret orders for Huáscar to be murdered.

In January 1533, Hernando was sent on an expedition to Pachacamac. In April, Diego de Almagro and reinforcements arrived from Panama. Pizarro bided his time, while his soldiers grew restless – they had come for conquest and spoils.

There remained the problem of Atahualpa. Despite incomplete fulfilment of his agreement, Pizarro absolved him of further obligation, but still held him – 'for security'. He was now an encumbrance; Pizarro wanted power and Atahualpa, now only a rallying point for native rebellion, stood in his way. De Almagro and his men wanted action and plunder. Rumours of native insurrection, the 'demands' of his

men and the Spanish Inquisition provided Pizarro with justification for a 'trial'. He and de Almagro were the judges. Atahualpa was accused of usurpation of the Inca throne and the murder of Huáscar the true heir, of inciting insurrection, of distributing gold and silver that should have been used to fulfil his ransom agreement and of adultery – as Sapas had numerous wives – and idolatry. He was convicted and condemned to be burned at the stake.

THE END OF INCA RULE

The final shameless act in these procedures followed. Twelve captains called the affair a travesty of justice, but were persuaded of its political expediency. When Atahualpa realized that he was to be burned, he agreed to be baptized a

Right: Despite this image, Atahualpa was strangled to death, after becoming a Christian to avoid being burned at the stake.

Christian for the favour of strangulation, for if he were burned, in Inca belief he would be condemned in afterlife, unable to be mummified and to continue to participate in life.

Pizarro finally marched to Cuzco and established Spanish government – a year after the events in Cajamarca. Alleged plans for insurrection by Challcuchima, one of Atahualpa's own generals, 'justified' his execution. A puppet Sapa, Manco, another of Huayna Capac's sons, was crowned. The last of Atahualpa's generals, Quizquiz, was defeated and fled to Quito, where he was killed by his own men.

The first years of Spanish rule were fraught with embittered rivalry between Pizarro, de Almagro and others. Pizarro enjoyed power for a mere eight years before being assassinated by rivals.

Below: The alleged 'ransom room' in Inca Cajamarca in which Atahualpa was imprisoned after being captured.

THE LAND

The continent of South America has a geography of extremes. Its mountains are some of the highest in the world – up to 7,000m (23,000ft); its deserts are some of the driest; its rainforests some of the wettest and densest; and its western offshore seas – the Humboldt Current – teem with some of the most abundant fisheries. Climates range from damp, steaming jungles to cold, dry deserts, and from cool, high plains to lofty, oxygen-rare summits. Rainfall can range from near zero to as much as 8,000mm (315in) a year.

Within this continent lies the Andean Area, which includes the two Cordilleras of the Andes, bordering the Amazon Rainforest on one side and the Atacama and other deserts on the other. Here humans have had to adapt to life at high altitudes. South of the Cordillera lies the Altiplano, where much of the area's farming is carried out. Here potatoes and other root crops were grown, and large herds of llamas kept for their wool. To the west lie coastal valleys and oases within the desert, where a variety of crops were grown.

East of the Andes is another world. The eastern mountain flanks descend more gradually through forested slopes, known as *montaña*, to the low, hot tropical forests, known as the selva. Here human settlement was more dispersed, yet products of the rainforest remained prominent in Andean and western coastal cultures throughout history.

Despite such extremes and a land of independent settlements, the Incas did not live in isolation: rather trade and social contact linked the settlements in both highlands and lowlands.

Left: The Callejon de Huaylas in north-central Peru epitomizes the sweeping slopes and high sierra valleys of the Andes.

PEAKS AND MOUNTAIN VALLEYS

The Andean Cordillera has been shaped in two distinct ways: by the movement of tectonic plates and by the weather.

FORMATION OF THE ANDES
Nearly two million years ago, the westward-moving South American continental plate met the eastward-moving Nazca ocean plate along the Pacific coast, moving at up to 15cm (6in) a year. The ocean plate, which has a heavier stone composition, was pushed beneath the lighter and less dense continental plate. Friction and drag where the two plates met caused folding, which created the Andean mountain chain. Where the ocean plate melted from the friction, the sedimentary rocks cracked, hurling molten rocks to the surface as volcanoes.

Below: Llamas, alpacas and vicuñas helped Andean civilizations to develop and survive in the Altiplano and high mountains.

Along their widest stretch, the spine of the Andes comprises two parallel ridges. On the east, the higher Cordillera Blanca borders the Amazon Rainforest. On the west, the Cordillera Negra fronts the Atacama Desert. South of this broad range the ridges diverge to flank, east and west, the broad Altiplano; to the north the mountains split into several ridges running parallel to the main ranges, and are cross-cut by shorter ridges to frame numerous sierra basins and valleys known as *puna*.

EFFECTS OF THE WEATHER
The distant Atlantic Ocean is the source of most of South America's precipitation. Westward-moving rain and snow meet the high Andes and fall on the eastern escarpments. West of the Andes, which lies in the rain shadow, a more arid Pacific weather pattern predominates. The Andes become drier as they become higher, and the Altiplano around the drainage of the

Above: In the challenging terrain of the sierra valleys and basins, rivers provided the vital water needed for agriculture.

Lake Titicaca basin forms a huge region of uninterrupted agricultural flatlands. Ninety per cent of Andean drainage runs east, ultimately to the Atlantic. Ten per cent drains into the Pacific, in numerous short, east–west-running river valleys from the western Andean flank.

The Andes also deflect prevailing ocean winds to blow north, causing the Pacific to flow northwards along the coast. Upwelling water from the deep tectonic trench brings cold, nutrient-rich and therefore seafood-rich currents, but also chills the air, so causing sparse rainfall.

A CHALLENGING ENVIRONMENT
The mountainous and highland regions of the Andes provide one of the most challenging environments on earth to their inhabitants. High mountain ecosystems are characteristically of low productivity, yet the majority of people in the central Andes live above 2,500m (8,200ft). Such altitudes comprise steep-sided valleys and basins, rugged terrains and a generally fragile landscape. Limited flat agricultural land, poor soils and a short growing season make production difficult. In addition, low oxygen levels, infrequent rainfall, high winds, high solar radiation and prevailing cold temperatures make survival tenuous.

Above: Mt Ausangate, in the central Peruvian Cordillera, was a typical abode of apu *spirits: sacred deities who inhabited the peaks.*

ADAPTING TO ALTITUDE

The high altitude causes stress on all life forms, and in humans, in particular, it decreases blood oxygen saturation by up to 30 per cent, which means breathing can be difficult for the unaccustomed. Andean peoples' bodies have, of course, become adapted to these conditions, with large chest cavities and lung capacity. Their cellular metabolism has modified to sustain higher red blood cell numbers. Nevertheless, strenuous work demands more energy to sustain the raised breathing, circulation and metabolic rates needed to maintain body temperature. As a result, highland peoples need to eat more to maintain a high basic metabolic rate, yet ironically they live in an environment where it is difficult to produce and obtain the necessary food for this diet.

The peopling of the Andes was thus a slow process, with generations at one altitude gradually becoming adapted to life at that level before their descendants could move into the next, higher zone, where the adaptive process took place again. Europeans, for the most part from comparatively lowland environments, have still been adapting through the generations since colonization began.

Unfortunately, we have no records of how lowland South Americans fared or coped with the high altitudes. Comparisons of the skeletons from lowland and highland burials, however, show that the two populations were more related within than between their respective groups.

POTATOES AND LLAMAS

In these highlands, agriculture consisted of a combination of root crops and herding. Because there are relatively few sizeable valleys – the valleys around Cuzco being exceptions – the steep slopes of valley and basin sides had to be adapted to provide flat areas for cultivation. Considerable labour and expertise were devoted to building millions of hillside terraces (*andenes*) and networks of irrigation canals.

The staple highland crop was the potato. Beans, squashes, peppers and peanuts were also important food crops. Maize can be grown at altitudes of up to 3,300m (11,000ft), but is at great risk from frost and hail at such heights.

The only domesticated animals were camelids (llamas, alpacas and vicuñas), dogs, guinea pigs and ducks. Llamas were herded in great flocks and provided the only pack animals for transport. They were also used for their wool (as were alpacas), meat and medicine. Dogs were raised as hunting companions and for food. Guinea pigs and ducks were raised for food, and also eggs in the case of the latter.

Below: Geographic map of the Andean Area, showing coastal plains, the Andes and the eastern rainforest.

ABUNDANT PLAINS – THE ALTIPLANO

The vast Altiplano (high plain) south of the central Peruvian Andes is formed where the principal Cordillera Blanca and Cordillera Negra diverge. Centred towards Lake Titicaca at the present Peruvian–Bolivian border, it lies at nearly 4,000m (13,000ft) above sea level. It forms a long trough, 800km (500 miles) north-west to south-east and drains north to south through a chain of lakes from Lake Azangaro in Peru through Titicaca to Lake Poopó in Bolivia. It is the largest expanse of agricultural flatlands in the Andean Area. The depth (up to 200m/650ft) and expanse (8,600 sq km/3,320 sq miles) of Lake Titicaca provides, as do the other lakes, a moderating influence on local temperatures.

In much of this region there was less need for labour-intensive terracing. Instead, pre-Hispanic peoples developed several methods for intensifying agricultural

Above: The sparser, bleaker high plains of the southern Altiplano provide little scope for agriculture, but they were widely used for llama herding.

production. Rivers were tapped by canals dug to channel their waters into the fields and to regulate ground water levels. In addition, check dams were constructed to collect and store run-off water, and aqueducts and dikes were made to divert and distribute it among the fields to water the crops.

CLAIMING THE LAND

During periods of high precipitation, the large region of low land, relatively speaking, around Lake Titicaca and the other lakes was reclaimed for agriculture by creating long, wide, ridged fields of mounded soils. They were separated by channels of slow-moving water, which provided protection from frost by releasing overnight the heat they had absorbed from the sun during the day. Nevertheless, to help maintain dense population levels, the steep slopes of the surrounding hills were also terraced to provide extra agricultural fields.

In drought years, when the lake level could drop by as much as 12m (39ft), some 50,000ha (124,000 acres) of formerly

Below: The high plains of the southern Andean plateaux are punctuated by volcanic cones, such as El Misti, believed to be the homes of gods whose destructive powers were feared.

Above: Alpacas were a species closely related to the llama. They provided a finer grade of wool than the llama.

cultivated land were left without the usual water channels and were simply abandoned temporarily.

As in the *puna*, the principal crops of the Altiplano were root vegetables. There were multiple varieties of potato, various tubers, legumes and grains such as quinoa domesticated from regional native species. In addition, the lakes, and especially Titicaca, provided a rich variety of aquatic resources. The deep, cold waters of the lakes supported abundant fish stocks, which had been exploited from early times. Migrating waterfowl (ducks and flamingos) provided plenty of seasonal meat and eggs. The shallow lakeshores harboured edible reeds – also used for roof thatching, clothing and for making fishing boats, and various water plants provided animal forage and were gathered as fodder for domesticated llama herds and guinea pigs.

GREAT HERDS OF LLAMAS

The llama and alpaca were both cornerstones of the Altiplano economy. Great herds of them were especially kept in the southern and northern Altiplano to sustain a pastoral way of life. From being the hunting grounds of the earliest inhabitants, these grasslands became the focus of llama and alpaca domestication from as early as 5000BC. Throughout the Andean

Area they were bred carefully for multiple purposes. The primary reason was for their wool, providing woven textiles for clothing, hats, bags and slings, as well as for exchange with lowland settlements for their produce. Textiles were also used to fulfil social taxation obligations.

As well as wool, several by-products were also of value. Llama meat and fat were important sources of protein and energy. Their bones were made into many tools, from scrapers, knives, needles and awls to musical instruments. The hides were made into clothing and other articles. Their dung was used as fuel and provided a source of fertilizer to re-enrich fields left fallow between growing seasons. Whole llamas were frequently sacrificed in religious ceremonies, and figured prominently in Andean cosmology. Finally, they were the pick-up trucks of pre-Hispanic Andeans, used to transport commodities over long distances.

Below: Vicuñas were prized for their fine wool and have adapted to high altitudes, where drought and freezing nights are the rule.

Above: Llamas were valuable, sure-footed pack animals for transporting goods between highlands and lowlands.

LIFE AT THE EDGE

Beyond the Altiplano lake basins, and especially towards the southern extreme of the great trough that forms the Altiplano, the landscape becomes increasingly arid. It would have been unsuitable for agriculture, or even llama herding, except in various isolated areas where a tenuous growing season could have been exploited with careful irrigation.

WESTERN DESERTS AND COASTAL VALLEYS

The western descent to the coastal strip of the Andean Area was an important and rich area of isolated cultural oases, at least in earliest pre-Hispanic times.

The region's climate is controlled by the Humboldt Current, which brings cold water northwards along the coast and creates cool, arid conditions inland. While the coastal air remains humid, causing coastal fog, temperature inversion (whereby air decreases in temperature less quickly than usual as it climbs) over the land inhibits rainfall and creates deserts inland – chiefly the Sechura in the north and the Atacama in the south of the Andean Area.

There is more arable land in the northern coastal valleys than in the southern coastal area. From north to south, there are three climate zones: semi-tropical in the north, sub-tropical in the middle and sub-tropical to desert in the south. The principal pre-Hispanic products of the coastal valleys and desert oases were maize, beans, squashes, peanuts, manioc, avocado and other semi-tropical fruits, and cotton.

Above: Eroding salt deposits of ancient raised shorelines are seen here at San Pedro de Atacama in Chile, the driest desert environment in the world.

IRRIGATION SYSTEMS

Along the Pacific watershed of the coastal strip virtually all desert farming and 85 per cent of sierra–coastal valley agriculture is reliant on run-off irrigation. More than 60 short rivers, rising in the steep western Andean slopes, descend through rugged then quickly levelling terrain to the Pacific Ocean. Tapping them for their water involved elaborate, labour-intensive projects to dig canals and channels to bring water from distant rivers to terraced fields. The very nature and sophistication of such works encouraged different regions to work together to establish and maintain them.

In the southern region of the coastal strip large expanses of desert provided a different challenge. Here people needed to bring water from the nearby sierra and from more widely spaced rivers. The Nazca and other rivers in this region flow on the surface in the upper

Left: Off-shore islands, such as Ballesta Island, Peru, were valuable sources of guano, used as fertilizer and a valuable trade item.

valleys only; down-valley they disappear into subterranean channels. In response to this condition, and perhaps enhanced in times of drought, the peoples of the area built elaborate underground irrigation systems of aqueducts to bring water from the underground rivers and to gather the water table through an arrangement of trenches and tunnels into catchment cisterns that could be tapped when needed.

HARVESTING THE SEA

In addition to agriculture, especially in the northern valleys (and largely independently from the southern desert valley agricultural societies), coastal cultures exploited the extremely rich maritime resources of the Pacific. Molluscs and crustaceans were collected on the foreshore; large and small fish were taken in nets and by hook (anchovies and sardines were harvested throughout the year and seasonally, respectively); sea mammals were hunted with harpoons; and sea birds were regularly taken. Offshore

islands, havens for vast seabird colonies, provided a regular source of guano for fertilizing the fields. Even edible kelp leaves were collected as a food source.

One commodity sought from farther north was the bivalve *Spondylus princeps* – the spiny or thorny oyster. Native in the coastal waters from Ecuador north to Baja California, it was exploited by coastal peoples from as early as 3000BC. Its collection is not easy, because its habitat is

Above: Vast deserts along the coasts of Peru and northern Chile contained scores of river valleys, providing oases for early agriculture.

18–50m (60–160ft) deep. Nevertheless, divers regularly collected it, and throughout pre-Hispanic times it provided a rich source of coastal and inland trade to both the north and south. It was sought as a ritual object and provides evidence of long-distance trade and contact between different cultures.

OASES CULTURES

In times of drought, oases cultures were stretched severely and it required, besides their religious beliefs, fortitude and ingenuity to sustain their cultural ways. Each river supplying an oasis valley, desert oasis or western sierra basin was otherwise isolated. Such isolation enabled several nearly self-governing populations to arise and maintain their independence. At the same time, however, there was a need for contact and the trading of goods from one region to another. Such links between desert oases, and indeed valleys, were spiritual and military enterprises whose strengths waxed and waned throughout Andean Area history.

Left: Ancient peoples of the desert coastlands relied on the rich harvest of the sea, and traded exotic shells with highland cultures.

THE *MONTAÑA* AND EASTERN RAINFORESTS

The geography of the eastern flank of the Altiplano and Cordillera provides a complete contrast to the western Cordillera. Here there are high, bleak plateaux called the *montaña* or Ceja de Selva, where the terrain and vegetation make agriculture difficult and careful terracing and water management are necessary. Llama herding is widespread here. Starting at about 4,000m (13,000ft) above sea level, the *montañas*, known as cloud forests, drop towards the east until they merge with true tropical forest. Rainfall averages 2,000–4,000mm (80–160in) a year.

RAINFOREST PRODUCTS

In addition to llama products, the hard and soft woods of the slopes provided the only major source of timber and wood for everyday and religious objects in the Andean Area. Agriculture on the middle slopes included maize, beans, squash, peanuts, peppers and cotton, all of which were transported by llama caravans specially commissioned by the rulers and elite of the Altiplano.

Most importantly, the *montaña* was the source of coca *(Erythroxylon coca)*, used for both practical and spiritual purposes. The alkaloid compounds derived from

Below: The stealth and power of the jaguar was revered by Andean peoples. It was a common 'form' for shape-changing shamans.

Above: The dense rainforests of Antisuyu were the source of many products, including hallucinogenic mushrooms.

the dried leaves of the coca plant or shrub provided (and continue to provide today) stimulation to relieve the fatigue of strenuous labour at high altitudes. It was also a ritual commodity of symbolic and real importance from very early times. Its importance and limited availability also encouraged political arrangements and even wars over its control. The true tropical rainforest lies mostly outside the Andean Area. Here precipitation can be in excess of 8,000mm (315in) per year, and it flows into rivers destined for the Atlantic Ocean. However, both the eastern *montaña* descending from the Altiplano and the north-eastern slopes from the northern Andes meet the Amazon Rainforest.

This closeness of *montaña* and rainforest encouraged cultural links, trade for rainforest products and a reverence for its creatures. The red, blue and yellow feathers of rainforest parrots, kingfishers and macaws were coveted by highland peoples. Harpy eagle feathers were also sought, and the bird's predatory nature admired. Cayman and serpent representations featured in much highland art and religious iconography, starting with the Chavín culture. Gold collected in placer mines, hallucinogenic plants (especially mushrooms and tobacco), resinous woods and various tropical fruits and medicinal plants all made their way to Andean cities. Jaguar pelts and monkeys were sought as both were revered animals whose cunning, courage, fierceness and cleverness was to be emulated.

THE LIMITS OF CIVILIZATION

The eastern boundaries of the Inca Empire extended to the edges of the Amazon. To the Incas this was the land of the Antisuyu quarter and the eastern edge of Collasuyu quarter, the place where civilization ended and savagery began. It was Inca Roca, the sixth Inca ruler, who defeated the Chunchos of Antisuyu only by adopting their savage tropical forest methods of fighting – he 'became' a jaguar and wore a green cloak. Viracocha, the eighth Sapa Inca, established the boundary between civilized highlands and savage Antisuyu when he destroyed the town of Calca 'with a fireball', 'propelling' it to the other side of the River Vilcanota. Manco Capac, the founding Inca – who was defined in legend as carrying maize, the highland, civilized crop – defeated the Hualla Indians in the Cuzco Valley. They were described as growers of rainforest crops such as peppers and coca.

The Incas made several attempts to conquer parts of the rainforest, but the environment proved too alien. Once within the forest, Inca generals lacked familiar points of reference on a visible horizon and their disorientated armies thrashed about in the dense, unfamiliar terrain. Pachacuti Inca Yupanqui, Tupac Yupanqui and Huayna Capac all sent campaigns into the jungles, and all were defeated. Despite this, bowmen from the *montaña* and tropical forest borders were recruited into the Inca army.

Above: Exotic rainforest birds provided the colourful feathers for ritual capes, tunics and headdresses made by skilled craftsmen.

A PLACE APART

To the Inca, the rainforest was *hurin*, feminine and subservient, despite their failure to conquer any of it or coerce any of its inhabitants into taxable submission. Ollantaytambo and Machu Picchu in Antisuyu defined the edge of Inca civilization, and one of their purposes in their border positions was to attempt to control coca production.

The trading relationship between highland cultures and tropical forest peoples was mostly one-way: from the tropical forest to the highlands. Although trade, both in commodities and ideas, was brisk at the borders, no serious attempts were made by highland peoples to colonize the rainforest or to establish large trading settlements at the borders. The rainforests remained in this passive role throughout pre-Hispanic history, providing precious raw materials, imagery and inspiration, but otherwise remaining a separate world.

Left: Winding rivers in the rainforest were home to the cayman, the South American crocodile, which inspired religious images.

LAND OF EXTREMES

The Andean Cordillera occupied by the Incas and their predecessors is an area of extremes, both environmental and ecological. They include the full global range of geographic landscapes and seascapes, from dense rainforests to teaming oceans. The Cordillera's inhabitants would have had to cope with fundamental contrasts in terrain, soil, water resources, sea, weather and temperature, depending on where they settled. Characteristically, though frustratingly for farmers, where there is adequate level land for cultivation there is often little water, and vice versa. Equally, seasonal and cyclical weather patterns mean that periods of regular rainfall, producing fertile growing conditions, are interspersed with periods of drought sometimes lasting years, decades or even centuries.

IRREGULAR RAINFALL

The mountainous landscape of the Cordillera means that rainfall is irregularly distributed. It is seasonal, starting about late October and November, climaxing between December and March and virtually disappearing from June to September. This annual cycle is decidedly irregular, however, swinging between values above and below the median, which occurs only about once every four years. This irregularity introduces another paradox in Andean survival. Rainfall for higher-altitude agriculture, where farmers devised methods to make more cultivatable land available, but where there is less water, generally fluctuates less. Yet run-off agriculture, which is generally more productive, is possible mostly where the rainfall fluctuates the most.

Highland farming is most successful when rainfall is heavy enough to cause sufficient run-off for crop production. (The run-off is stored in a structure of suitable size and construction and used to water the land during dry periods.) But arid mountain soils absorb fixed amounts of moisture, and so run-off occurs only when this absorption level is exceeded. Rainfall exceeding this capacity generally occurs only between about 3,900m (12,800ft) and 4,900m (16,100ft). Above about 5,000m (16,400ft) most available water is locked-up in glaciers and ice fields. Therefore, severe fluctuations in rainfall in this crucial altitudinal zone have a severe effect on the amount of

Above: The Incas conquered the parched, desiccated surface of the Atacama and other western coastal deserts.

run-off water available down-slope in the most important agricultural basins and valleys. This unbalanced relationship between rainfall and run-off also explains the dramatic variation of the rivers of the Pacific coastal valleys.

STRESSFUL CONDITIONS

The effects of living at high altitude and coping with low blood oxygen saturation made life stressful for early Andeans. They needed to eat more than lowlanders to maintain their metabolic rate, yet changeable weather patterns and scarce foodstuffs made life precarious. Supporting and sustaining civilization in highland regions was thus measurably more costly in many ways than it was in lowland areas.

Alongside the daily stresses of living, earth movements and weather cycles caused problems. Tectonic activity, both small and large scale, brings disastrous consequences. Relentless tectonic creep exacerbates erosional patterns and affects canals and water collection methods by altering slopes, damaging canals and affecting their performance.

Left: The lush, well-watered Amazonian rainforest proved to be too alien and disorientating to the Inca armies.

Sudden disaster also came from earthquakes and volcanoes. Shifts from the plates that formed the Andes brought an earthquake of magnitude 7 or greater on the Richter Scale about once a decade. The immediate effects and consequent landslides caused fatalities as well as damage to buildings, canals and other structures. Volcanic activity persisted throughout ancient times, and into the present, especially in the northern Andean Area in Ecuador, southern Colombia and the Vicanota region of southern Peru.

Unable to explain these events scientifically, peoples of the Andes developed their own spiritual explanations involving cosmic battles and angry gods. Even into modern times they believed in mountain gods. When Mount Huaynaputina in southern Peru erupted in AD1600, the power of the explosion blew the entire crown of the mountain away, leaving a huge crater. Natives believed the event to be a rebellion of the ancient deities against the victory of the Christian gods.

Below: The sierra valleys were well watered but challenging. Raised fields and terracing maximized the amount of level ground for crops.

THE DREADED EL NIÑO

The phenomenon known as El Niño disrupted even what could be regarded as the 'regular' rainfall cycles described above, introducing perennial episodes of hostsile weather conditions. El Niños occur about every four to ten years. They are caused by the warming of the eastern tropical Pacific, changing atmospheric conditions, and altering weather cycles in the far and central Pacific. The conditions

Above: The high sierra provided abundant water for mountain valleys and oases, as well as mountain gods and burial places.

also act to magnify the effects of changes in solar radiation. Usually lasting about 18 months, El Niños generate torrential storms accompanied by cataclysmic floods along the western coasts. Simultaneously, because the weather patterns have been reversed, the mountains and Altiplano become subject to prolonged periods of drought.

Along the desert western coasts, tonnes of debris deposited by earthquake-induced landslides, having lain loose for years, are flushed into the sea in the floods. Ground into fine sands by wave action, it is redeposited along the beaches. Strong offshore winds then collect it into huge dunes that can choke the life out of cities and settlements far inland.

Even longer-term droughts and wet periods affected Cordillera civilization. Evidence from glacier ice shows a substantial increase in atmospheric dust caused by drought between *c.*2200 and 1900BC; other extended droughts occurred in 900–800BC, 400–200BC, AD1–300, 562–95 and 1100–1450. Wetter periods occurred in AD400–500, 900–100 and 1500–1700.

LIVING WITHIN THE LANDSCAPE

Andean cultures faced great challenges, many of which were presented by the landscape around them. With its high mountains, dense rainforests and arid deserts, much of the Andean Area was not suitable for habitation, but, even so, communities developed wherever they could.

ESTABLISHING LINKS

Most early Andean communities developed in isolated situations in the western coastal valleys, the desert oases and the basins that lay between the mountains. Surrounding terrain made such settlements, by their very nature, independent and self-sufficient for the essentials of life.

Despite their isolation, however, such communities began to make contact with peoples in other regions and from other cultures. This may have been instigated as much by curiosity as by a desire to foster trade in order to supplement limited foodstuffs and other goods. As these links became established, social contact and trade took place across long distances. Inca civilization, as the empire was expanded, developed and exploited long-established patterns of long-distance trade.

Below: Maize was grown on the north coast of South America and throughout the Andean Area at 2,000–3,000m (6,600–9,800ft).

CONTRADICTORY CONDITIONS

Successful agriculture in the Cordillera and the development of civilization relied upon adequate sunshine, favourable temperatures, fertile soil, arable land and sufficient water – and also on the presence/availability of domesticated plants and animals.

In the *punas*, where agricultural settlements were carefully managed, the ruggedness and steepness of the land, along with poor weather conditions, increase with altitude, making the lower slopes the obvious places to develop. Yet in times of drought, mountain precipitation and soil moisture shift up-slope by 100–400m

Above: This burial mantle displays a religious motif of mountain pumas or rainforest jaguars, from whose tails dangle trophy heads.

(320–1,300ft) above normal distribution, leaving these lower slopes arid. Claiming and maintaining drought-tolerant ground for agricultural purposes required massive investments in materials and labour to check the erosion of thin mountain soils on steep slopes and to direct water to fields and terraces, and considerable will and co-operation to accomplish it.

The dramatically different environmental conditions between highlands and lowlands described earlier in this chapter

clearly reinforced the economic and cultural differences among the mountain, maritime-oasis, and *montaña* and rainforest peoples.

Each region in the Andean Area had strengths and weaknesses to encourage, challenge or inhibit its inhabitants. During periods of regional settlements, these varying strengths encouraged cultural variety. Yet, at the same time, the most important river valleys were centres for the spread of cultural developments that unified different regions. Prominent examples include the Chavín culture from its mountain valley, the Moche people in the Lambayeque and adjacent northern coastal valleys, the Nazca culture from its southern coastal desert oasis, the Wari and Tiwanaku 'empires', respectively in the high Cordillera and the Altiplano, and the Incas from their central Andean mountain valley.

Sierra basins and east–west-running river valleys of the western coast form self-sufficient oases for settlements. Steep mountain gorges, high passes and dry deserts make access between regions difficult and inhibit contact between their

Below: The potato provided a staple of the Andean diet. It was cultivated at elevations of 2,000 to nearly 4,000m (6,600–13,100ft).

inhabitants, separating and segregating rather than uniting them. Vast amounts of effort would have been needed to incorporate large areas into states and kingdoms, as occurred throughout Andean prehistory.

The periods of drought described above affected farming reliant on run-off water much more than agriculture reliant on direct rainfall. This was because arid, absorbent mountain soils better retained the moisture available. Alternating wetter periods brought greater benefit to run-off agriculture and coastal irrigation schemes because of the reversals of the 'normal' distributions of weather patterns and precipitation.

REDISTRIBUTION OF ASSETS

Cultivation reliant on run-off water normally provides higher yields than rainfall farming. Thus, the vast plains of the Altiplano were exploited with raised fields, and the western coastal valley and desert oases with re-channelled water from the rivers. Both areas developed joint labour schemes to build the necessary structures. Such methods secured more arable land at high altitudes than in the lowlands, but, frustratingly, only about 20 per cent of Andean cultivated crops grow well above 3,000m (9,800ft), while 90 per cent grow best below 1,000m (3,300ft), so there is a limit on how much production increases.

Above: The transport of goods by llama caravans enabled trading between lowland and highland regions to take place.

These differences in the distribution of productive land, crops and resources led to the development of relations between regions to the point that they were dependent upon each other. Raw materials and products were exchanged through trade from very early times, but also through conquest and coercion. During periods of unity, not only were produce and rare commodities traded between coast and mountain, and between mountain and *montaña* and rainforest, but also the ruling elite actually redistributed groups of people to moderate the effects of adverse seasonal weather patterns. These practices are well documented for the Inca, and archaeological evidence from earlier cultures, kingdoms and empires indicates that such practices were developed much earlier.

The redistribution of both goods and labour enabled rulers to maintain control by making sure that everyone under their rule had sufficient resources to live on. To such an end, the Incas used llama caravans to take produce and manufactured goods between highlands and lowlands. Potatoes, maize, peanuts, chilli peppers, coca leaves and much else were transported in woollen and cotton sacks in llama caravans.

SACRED LANDSCAPES, SACRED SKIES

The ancient Andean cultures revered every aspect of their environment: the landscape and seascape, and the very skies above them. Unable to explain their universe scientifically, ancient Andeans, like other ancient peoples, explained their surroundings with reconstruction stories that were rooted in their view of the world.

The Milky Way, known as Mayu, was thought to be *the* celestial river, and thus the source of all moisture – a vital part of Andean life. Mayu also had important influences on daily life, and the Incas formed links between the stars in the sky and myths. They also formed a view of a cyclical world.

Nature was considered a living, breathing being. It was something to engage with rather than to conquer, to co-operate with rather than to dominate. The landscape and skies were animate and charged with interactive, reciprocal forces.

There were many sacred places called *huacas* within the Andean Area. Most *huacas* were natural places, but others were man-made or were human modifications of natural work. Mountain tops, known as *apus*, were also venerated, although volcanoes and earthquakes were more feared for their destructive powers – the anger of the gods.

Further elements of mystery are added to the Andean landscape by Nazca lines, forming natural figures and shapes in the desert, and *ceque* lines – sacred pathways radiating from Cuzco.

Left: Mt Illimani, in the Cordillera Real, and other peaks were believed to be the source of water and the homes of the gods.

PLACES OF WORSHIP

To the Incas, and no doubt to their Andean Area ancestors, their entire surroundings were sacred. Throughout the landscape, special places that had been revered for generation after generation, and where offerings were made or special rituals performed, were known as *huacas*. As well as the powerful central deities of the Inca pantheon, whose presences were manifested in individual temples in the Coricancha in Cuzco, Andean peoples recognized a host of lesser nature gods, spirits and oracles that existed throughout the land. *Huacas* were places where such lesser figures could also be revered and, if necessary, placated.

INCA *HUACAS*

Huacas were hallowed places where significant mythological events had taken place and/or where offerings were made to local deities. It is thought that all Andean cultures had *huacas* that were special to them, and thus most *huacas* were of ancient origin. The majority were natural

Below: The sacred Intihuatana (Hitching Post of the Sun) at Machu Picchu typifies natural outcrops carved as sacred huacas.

features of the landscape, such as mountaintops (*apus*), caves, springs and especially stones or boulders, but they could also be man-made objects, or natural objects or landscape features modified by human workmanship. An Inca *huaca* could also be a location along a sacred *ceque* line (a sacred route), such as the pillars erected on the western horizon above Cuzco for viewing the sunset from the Capac Usnu for special astronomical observations.

In and around Cuzco there were more than 300 *huacas*. Other Inca sacred places were concentrated wherever there was an association with a ruler. For example, Huayna Capac, the twelfth Sapa Inca, undertook a special pilgrimage to visit the favourite places of his father, Tupac Yupanqui, in Cajamarca, as did Atahualpa those of Huayna Capac in the northern provinces before marching against his brother Huáscar. Ironically, it was in Cajamarca that Atahualpa met defeat at the hands of Pizarro.

Ceque lines themselves, by their very nature as sacred or ritual pathways, were also *huacas*, and, equally, they incorporated *huacas* as points along the sacred routes they provided.

Above: The outcrop of Qenqo, north of Cuzco, was one of the Inca's most sacred huacas. *It resembles a seated puma.*

ANCESTRAL *HUACAS*

Royal and elite mausoleums, where the mummified remains of ancestors were kept, were also regarded as *huacas*. Spanish colonial sources identify many Inca royal *huacas*; and Chan Chan, the capital of the rulers of Chimú, surrounded their royal mausoleum compounds. These records reveal what appear to be the two basic classifications of such man-made *huacas*: the *huacas adatorios* – the sanctuaries and temples where gods and goddesses were worshipped; and the *huacas sepulturas* – the burial places of the most important members of the deceased.

A characteristic *huaca* is the collection of stones known as the Pururaucas around Cuzco. These were revered as the re-petrified ancient stones that had allegedly risen up and become Inca warriors to help Pachacuti Inca Yupanqui defend Cuzco against the Chancas in the early 15th century. Other examples include Qenqo, just north of Cuzco, where one large

Above: Stone cairns on mountain passes were a special type of huaca *called an* apacheta. *They were thought to hold local deities' spirits.*

upright boulder was left untouched, presumably because its silhouette resembled that of a seated puma, and the sacred shrines and statues of Viracocha at Cacha and Urcos. In some cases a *huaca* was a combination of the natural and the miraculous. Once again the stones of Pururaucas are a prime example. Another is the stone of the ancestor brother Ayar Uchu atop Huanacauri Mountain, which is believed to be the petrified body of that ancestor. Yet another example is Pariacaca, which/who seems to have been simultaneously a mountain and a mobile deity or culture hero.

PROVINCIAL *HUACAS*
The movements and final resting places of important rulers strengthened attachments to the natural symbolism of *huacas* as ancestral or 'parental'. The hill called Huanacauri above Cuzco, for example, was regarded as the father of three of the founding Inca ancestors, each turned to stone as a prominent rock or crag. Other Andean

peoples regarded the local mountains as being 'like parents' who gave birth to the local community. Indeed, such beliefs are enshrined in the story of the creation of peoples by the god Viracocha, who assigned each people their region as a sacred act.

Most tribes, 'nations' and towns undoubtedly had a particular place that was recognized as their group's *huaca*. Equally, most kinship groups, the *ayllus*, also had their own *huacas*. It was believed that the spirit of the *huaca* exerted a special influence over the lives and destinies of the members of the group. *Huacas* continue to be recognized by local peoples in the Andes today in a mixture of pre-Christian and Catholic belief.

LINKS FROM PAST TO PRESENT
Reverence at *huacas* and the following of *ceque* lines represented a strengthening of the past, a reassurance of the present and an insuring of the future. Indeed, the myth-history attached to Inca sacred places infused the very landscape.

The stories attached to individual *huacas* have survived mostly in fragments. Many are recoverable, however, from traditions transcribed in the longer narratives

of Inca history. Although the sacred *huaca* system is well known in and around Cuzco, there is less surviving direct evidence of other local shrines; but much may still be discovered through further research.

Below: All rivers and lakes were held sacred by ancient Andeans because water was universally recognized as the source of life.

SACRED WATERS

Water was vital to the Incas and their predecessors, and as such was revered almost as a god. They believed the cosmos itself to include a celestial ocean upon which the Earth floated.

CELESTIAL RIVER

The Milky Way, Mayu, was *the* celestial river, counterpart to all earthly rivers and the source of all moisture. Water from the sea was collected into Mayu, flowed into and across the sky and was released as rain and snow on the mountains to fill the streams, rivers and lakes, flow into the sea, and form as dew, frost, mist and fog on the land and over the ocean. From small runnels developed the mountain streams and rivers that watered the landscape. Humans then exercised the utmost ingenuity to make the most of the collection of water and use it to water crops.

Inca records transcribed in the Spanish sources describe how Andean farmers followed Mayu's movements carefully, for the solstices of the Milky Way coincide with the beginnings of the wet and dry seasons. Weather patterns, however, were

Below: The River Urubamba was a major source of irrigation in the central Andes and one of the most sacred rivers.

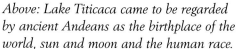

periodically disrupted by El Niño events, causing long periods of drought in areas where regular seasonal rain had made the land fertile. Such times were very difficult for people in the western sierra, valley and desert oases, mountain basins and the Altiplano.

Such careful observation and the invention of an explanation of the seasonal associations demonstrates the seamless link in the pre-Hispanic Andean mind between the practical necessity of water and the sacred origin of it. In addition to its strictly practical uses, water played an

Above: Lake Titicaca came to be regarded by ancient Andeans as the birthplace of the world, sun and moon and the human race.

important role in religious ritual. Andean peoples reliant on rainwater for their agricultural survival made offerings to the natural forces through the deities that controlled them. By 'feeding' the gods in this way, they created a reciprocal obligation, which, it was hoped, would secure a reliable supply of water.

HIDDEN WATERS

This sacred and practical association began with the earliest Andean civilizations. In religious ceremonial centres, water clearly played an important part and was used to complement ritual. U-shaped temples were oriented towards mountain sources of water. At Chavín de Huántar, an intriguing aspect of the galleries and passages within its temples is the apparent acoustic use of water within its hidden interior. The system of conduits to the chambers could literally be made to roar when water was flushed rapidly through the drains and the sound vented around the chambers. What this sounded like and what feelings it evoked in the hearts and minds of worshippers in the courtyards outside can only be imagined.

In the Early Intermediate Period, the Nazca culture inhabiting the dry desert landscape of the southern Peruvian coast naturally found the capture, collection and use of water paramount to their survival. One of the functions of their geoglyphs was the promotion and maintenance of communication with distant mountain deities who controlled the flow of water. For geological reasons, the Nazca River (and others in this drainage system) disappears into subterranean channels at mid-valley. The site of the ceremonial centre of Cahuachi in the mid-Nazca River drainage area appears to have been deliberately placed between the two zones of surface water flow. Residential settlements up and down the valley apparently used Cahuachi as their sacred gathering place for worship. Underground cisterns connected by aqueducts and reached by stone-cobbled spiral paths formed a system of water supply and control.

Below: The sacredness of water was encapsulated in channels and fountains in Inca cities, as here at Machu Picchu.

THE PUMA'S TAIL

Given the earlier Andean preoccupation with the importance of water, it is no coincidence that one-third of the sacred *ceque* pathways around Cuzco led to or were otherwise oriented by the major springs and other sources of water in the region. When Pachacuti Inca Yupanqui rebuilt Cuzco after securing Inca supremacy in the valley, the Huatanay and Tullumayu rivers were partly re-routed to conform to the new plan of the city – that of a crouching puma. At the south-east end of the city, where the two rivers converge, the triangular patch of land thus created forms the puma's tail.

Above: The zigzag water channel cut into the natural outcrop at Qenqo branches, then rejoins. It was used for ritual libations.

SACRED TITICACA

The sacredness of water in pre-Hispanic Andean civilization is most fundamentally shown in the singular reverence for Lake Titicaca as the place of origin. The focus of the Tiwanaku Empire in the Early Intermediate Period and Middle Horizon, Titicaca was regarded as the legendary place of the origin of the cosmos. Peoples throughout the Andes created myths and legendary historical links to establish their origin at Titicaca/Tiwanaku.

MOUNTAINS OF THE GODS

In a land dominated by dramatic landscapes, it was inevitable that mountains and their features and characteristics became the focus of awe and were imbued with divine powers. Mountains were regarded as the dwelling places of the gods or even as the gods themselves. They were associated with weather patterns and recognized as the ultimate source of water.

SACRED MOUNTAIN LOCATIONS
Among the mountains there were several special types of *huacas*. A stone or stones regarded as the petrified ancestor of a people or *ayllu* was known as a *huanca*. Especially prominent or large boulders in the landscape, which were believed to incorporate the essence of an ancestor of one or more local kinship groups, were typical examples of *huancas*. Such *huancas* were (and still are) to be found in town centres or placed upright in the middle of a field. As the physical

Below: The primeval Moche mountain god, also associated with the creator god Ai Apaec, is depicted at the Huaca de la Luna.

manifestation or representation of an ancestor, they were thought to act as a guard on the interests of the local community.

The *apacheta* comprised a pile of stones at the top of a mountain pass or at a crossroads. *Apachetas* were believed to hold the spirits of local deities, and travellers would seek the favour of these gods by leaving offerings of coca leaves (*Erythroxylon coca*, the source of cocaine) or clothing, or by adding a stone to the heap before continuing their journeys. In a practical way, such features also no doubt acted as way-markers for travellers unsure of the route ahead.

With virtually every mountainscape dominated by volcanic peaks, they were only too evident as sources of mysterious power. Such special *huacas* were venerated as *apu* (literally 'lord') and were believed to have a direct influence on animal and crop fertility for those who lived in their vicinity. Sacred pilgrimages to such mountaintops to seek the favour of the spirit of the *apu* were a regular feature of Andean traditional religion – a long-standing practice that continues to the present day.

Above: The Late Intermediate Period Sicán Tucume pyramid in the Lambayeque Valley mimicked the shape of a mountain.

THE PRIMEVAL MOUNTAIN GOD
The concept of a god of the mountains was one of the most ancient aspects of Andean civilization. In one of his earlier manifestations, as the mountain god of the Moche, he was recognized as both a creator and sky god, but was believed to have played only a remote part in human affairs. He thus remained nameless but was represented frequently on Moche pottery and textiles with feline features. The depiction of images of fanged beings on Chavín pottery of much earlier date might have been his prototype, and thus the concept of a divine mountain power was spread far and wide.

The obvious association of mountains and the weather was reflected in the close association of the mountain god and Ai Apaec, sky god or perhaps son. The mountain god's throne was usually placed on a mountaintop, beneath which his manifestation as Ai Apaec was more active in association with terrestrial affairs. Moche military conquest and/or ritual combat was partly undertaken for the purpose of taking prisoners for sacrifice to these deities. According to some authorities, Ai Apaec was also the principal god of the Chimú of the Late Intermediate Period, derived from the Moche culture. Others argue that Ai Apaec simply means 'to make', and was therefore an invisible creator comparable to later Inca Viracocha.

Above: Volcanoes were recognized as the homes of the gods, whose anger with humans was also shown by destructive earthquakes.

VOLCANOES AND EARTHQUAKES

Volcanic eruptions, although not frequent occurrences, were seen as the wrath of the gods, not necessarily as punishment for wrong-doing in a retributional sense, but rather simply as demonstrations of how much the fate of humankind was in the hands of the gods. Earthquakes were even more prominent in this role and were perhaps equal in importance only to water and the sun in influencing Andean civilization.

Earthquakes disrupted the very framework of civilization, wreaking great physical damage and affecting the fabric of society and its organization. Reliance on water and its careful redirection and distribution from mountains to agricultural terraces paradoxically left the dependants knowingly vulnerable to the destruction of the terraces by the very deities who provided the water and who dwelled at its source.

Cyclopean architecture and the close-fitting blocks of Inca architecture also reflect the influence of earthquakes. Built to withstand seismic shocks, Inca architecture is often more stable than the Spanish colonial and later structures that replaced it or were built on Inca foundations. Perhaps even the fact that so many *huacas* are stones was influenced by earthquakes: such natural formations, as part of the landscape often not destroyed in earthquakes, may have been perceived to be one of the immutable elements of cosmic structure.

A principal god of earthquakes was Pachacamac, synonymous with and worshipped at one of the most ancient sites of Andean civilization. The site and the god rivalled the Island of the Sun in Lake Titicaca for supremacy as the most sacred location of the Andean Area. Pachacamac was the Earth-shaker – even the most minor tremor was a reminder of his presence and power. In recognition and reverence, Pachacuti Inca Yupanqui assumed the name of Earth-shaker after his defeat of the Chancas and domination of the Cuzco Valley.

THE INFLUENCE OF MOUNTAINS

The divinity of mountains also influenced the architecture of ancient Andean civilizations. From earliest times, U-shaped temple structures were oriented to the mountains, perhaps opening their arms to the divine powers and pleading for the water they provided. Pyramidal temple structures seemed to mimic in miniature the mountains around them, and yet themselves still dwarfed the humans who built them, seemingly reminding them of their powerlessness in the hands of the gods. The fabric of many pyramidal mounds, which were built of millions of adobe (mud) bricks, is the result of the mixing and moulding together of both earth and water – the two fundamental mountain elements.

The sacredness of mountains and their power over the survival of civilization remained a feature throughout Inca times. Llibiac, a god of thunder and lightning, was the principal deity of the Llacuaz Ayllu of Cajatambo – showing the continuity of belief and its interconnection with Andean social organization.

A final and rather poignant reminder of mountain-top sacredness is the use of remote mountain peaks as the place of child sacrifice in Inca times. In recent years the discovery of the freeze-dried mummies of some of these sacrifices has provided some of the most spectacular and informative evidence of pre-Hispanic religious practices.

Below: Mt Ausangate in the Cordillera Central was the personification of the apu *sacred mountain spirit.*

LINES IN THE DESERT

The coastal desert *pampa* of southern Peru was the home of the Nazca culture, which flourished from about 200BC to AD500. All aspects of Nazca culture were dominated by ritual. Perhaps the most dramatic evidence of this was the making of lines and images in the desert in the form of geoglyphs. Many people have investigated the lines and their meaning over decades, including Paul Kosok, Maria Reiche and Anthony Aveni.

Other line figures were made in the Pacific coastal valleys from Lambayeque to northern Chile.

SHAPES IN THE DESERT

The Nazca desert lines are the most famous examples of pre-Inca sacred routes. The lines, which can be best seen and most appreciated from the air, were made by scraping the patinated desert surface gravel and stones to one side to reveal the lighter coloured, unpatinated under-surface. The lines are formed by

Below: The sacred route at Cantalloc on the Nazca Desert plain of southern Peru typifies a geometric geoglyph in its spiral pathway.

the combination of light sand and aligned gravel and stones. The region's natural aridity has helped to preserve them.

More than 640 sq km (425 sq miles) of the desert are covered with these lines, figures and shapes. They comprise recognizable figures, geometrical shapes and seemingly random lines and cleared areas. Recognizable figures are of animals revered in the Nazca religious concept of the world – spiders, monkeys and birds – plus flowers and human-like supernatural figures. Some lines run perfectly straight

Above: The Giant of Atacama at Cerro Unitas, northern Chile, is the world's largest hill figure at 86m (280ft) high.

for great distances across the desert. Others spiral, or converge on a single point. Altogether there are some 1,300km (800 miles) of such lines.

FIGURES AND PATTERNS

There are two principal types or groups. Figures on low slopes or hillsides seem to be placed such that they are obvious to travellers on the plains below, even though seen obliquely. Patterns of lines, both straight and curving, form 'enclosed' or designated areas, geometric shapes and large cleared patches.

Sets of lines form geometric patterns, and clusters of straight lines converge on common nodes, or, conversely, radiate from 'ray centres' on hills. In his researches, the archaeo-astronomer Anthony Aveni has identified and mapped 62 such nodes and radiations. Some of the lines lead to irrigated oases, or link sites, such as the line between the settlement of Ventilla and the ritual centre of Cahuachi. Individual straight lines of various widths are more than 20km (12½ miles) long. One famous set of lines, which forms a huge arrow of 490m (roughly 1,600ft), pointing towards the Pacific Ocean, is thought to be a symbol to invoke rain.

Each animal or plant figure comprises a single continuous line, with different beginning and ending points. The line never crosses itself. There is a humming-bird, a duckling, a spider, a killer whale, a monkey, a llama, several plants and human-like beings, as well as trapezoids and triangles of cleared areas, zigzags and spirals. Altogether there are some 300 such figures, and, combined with the lines, about 3.6 million sq m (10.8 million sq ft) of *pampa* floor have been scraped away to create them.

MYSTERIOUS LINES?

The Nazca figures are difficult to conceive, and certainly impossible to see as whole figures from the ground, except obliquely. Their presence has prompted a variety of speculation regarding their meaning, and argument has raged for more than 60 years over the meanings of these and other geoglyphs. Proposals range from their having been made by beings from outer space – for which there is categorically no evidence – to their use for astronomical observation – which seems plausible but has not yet been conclusively demonstrated.

There is no evidence that the lines were made by anyone other than the Nazca themselves. Although we will never know the exact meaning of each line or figure, they are clearly ritual lines,

Below: The great hummingbird geoglyph on the Nazca Desert plain represents a messenger from the gods.

shapes and figures that reflect Nazca religious concepts. Their similarity to patterns on pottery and textiles, associations with Nazca burials and mummification, and with Nazca settlements and water sources reflects Nazca cosmology.

Creating the lines was a simple matter of proportional geometry. There is no difficulty in tracing an envisioned figure in the sand, and then translating the shape into a giant figure on the ground: only multiplication and proportional ratios are necessary to replicate a drawing using strings and pegs to trace and pace out the positions of the lines and patterns. Straight lines that cross the desert are easily produced by aiming at fixed positions on the horizon. Practical experiments to make neo-Nazca lines have proved the ease with which they can be created and the relatively small number of people and time needed to do so.

WHAT WERE THEY USED FOR?

The most plausible, and indeed obvious, explanation of the meaning of the Nazca lines is linked to the landscape, climate and accompanying features of Nazca settlement and material culture. The lines were associated with the Nazcas' necessary preoccupation with water and the fertility of their crops, together with the worship of mountains – the ultimate source of irrigation waters – and a pantheon of deities

Above: The geoglyph at Paracas, southern Peru, might have been a symbol of desert fertility and an orienteering aid to fishermen.

or supernatural beings who were believed to be responsible for bringing or with-holding the rains.

Some lines may be related to astro-nomical observations – especially the positions of the sun through the year – that reflect times for planting and harvesting. Geometric patterns are ritual pathways, created and owned by groups within Nazca social organization for ceremonial processions. Ceremony, praying to the gods for the elements of life itself, is part of the 'mystery' of the lines. The axes of most lines run parallel to watercourses. Other lines are just as clearly the paths between settlements and the ceremonial centres themselves.

The number of lines, and their creation over a period of 700–800 years, over-marking each other in great profusion, shows that they were not conceived as a grand overall plan. The lines and figures appear to have been made by and for small groups – perhaps even individuals. Some may have been created for a single ceremony; others were used repeatedly. 'Solid' cleared areas might have been for congregations, while figures probably formed ritual pathways to be walked by people for specific ritual purposes.

CEQUE PATHWAYS

The *ceque* system of sacred routes was a uniquely Inca theoretical and practical concept interwoven with myth, astronomical observation, architectural alignment, and the social and geographical divisions of the empire. Sacred routes, however, were vital parts of pre-Inca cultures as well, and in this light the Inca *ceque* lines can be seen as integral with a long tradition of systems of sacred routes and pathways dating from pre-Hispanic Andean culture.

Ceques were straight, sacred 'lines' radiating from the Coricancha sacred precinct in Cuzco. Each line linked numerous *huacas* along its length. There were 41 such lines uniting 328 *huacas* and survey points within and around Cuzco. It is perhaps significant that the 328 *huacas* and stations correspond to

Below: Map showing the ceque *system of sacred or ritual routes linking the shrines and their locations.*

the number of days in the 12 sidereal lunar months (328/12 = the 27.3-day period of the rotation of the moon around the Earth–moon centre of mass). They were grouped according to 'upper' (*hanan*) and 'lower' (*hurin*) Cuzco and thus to the four quarters of the empire. Although theoretically straight, for practical purposes *ceques* sometimes had to obey the restrictions of the actual terrain through which they ran.

MULTIPLE PURPOSES

Points along the lines also served to regulate land holdings, water distribution, labour divisions, and ritual and ceremonial activities. *Ceques* were used as processional routes followed by *capacocha (*sacrificial individuals) at the beginnings of their journeys to the place of sacrifice. Combinations of *ceques* and their associated *huacas* distinguished the different *panaca* kin-group land-holdings within Inca society.

Above: Inca roads followed valley routes between cities, crossing mountain passes and river gorges using grass-fibre bridges.

For example, sunset on 26 April and the observation of the setting of the Pleiades on or about 15 April were made from the same place in the Capac Usnu plaza in central Cuzco. The settings were viewed between two stone pillars, together regarded as a *huaca*, which had been erected on the skyline west of the city. Farther on, beyond the horizon, another *huaca* was the spring named Catachillay, another name for the Pleiades.

The movements of Mayu, the Milky Way, were linked to the *ceque* system by a division separating the four quarters along the inter-cardinal (between-the-compass-points) axis of Mayu, and the southernmost point of Mayu's movement in the night sky.

The 16th-century Spanish chronicler Juan de Betanzos describes the sixth *ceque* of Antisuyu quarter, on which lay the sixth *huaca*, as 'the house of the puma'. Here the mummified body of the wife of the emperor Pachacuti Inca Yupanqui was kept, to whom child sacrifices were offered.

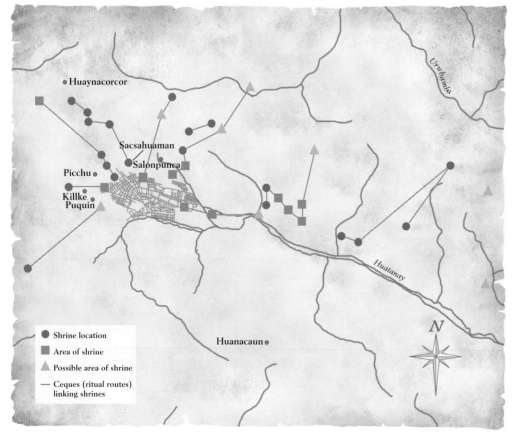

Shrine location
Area of shrine
Possible area of shrine
Ceques (ritual routes) linking shrines

Huaynacorcor

Sacsahuaman

Salonpunca

Picchu

Killke
Puquin

Huatanay

Urubamba

Huanacaun

N

CEQUES AND SOCIAL STRUCTURE

Once again it was the vital importance of water in Andean life that formed an important part in the creation and use of the *ceque* ritual routes. The four *suyus* (quarters) of the Inca Empire, represented in the four divisions of Cuzco, were demarcated by the organization of the flow of water through the city. In turn, the radiating *ceque* lines organized the kinship *ayllu* groups into a hierarchy of positions either up or down river. This hierarchy itself reflected the nature of Inca society, in which different *ceque* lines were associated with the different bloodlines, particularly with the royal *panacas*, each of which was the origin of one of the primary descendants of the Inca ruler.

Thus, each *ceque* was created by and held information about irrigation, the Inca calendar and religious worship. Each *ceque* and its functions were maintained and tended by the appropriate kinship group

and social rank – aristocratic, mixed-blood or common – in a rotational system as the *ceque* lines were marked off around the horizon surrounding Cuzco.

In his *Historia del Nuevo Mundo*, Bernabé de Cobo describes the eighth *ceque* in the Chinchaysuyu (north-west quadrant). At its seventh *huaca*, a hill called Sucanca, a channel brought water from Chinchero. Two towers erected on the hill marked the position of the rising sun on the day when maize planting had to begin. Consequently, sacrifices at the *huaca* were directed to the sun, soliciting him to appear and shine through the towers at the appropriate time.

The system of *ceque* lines also regulated the Inca organization of annual labour, especially seasonal labour to do with agriculture and the maintenance of irrigation systems. Once a year, in the central plaza of upper (*hurin*) Cuzco, a ritual ploughing took place. Chosen representatives from 40 families selected from the four quarters dug up as if for planting a designated portion of the plaza field. Such a system of shared civic responsibilities and duties in prearranged patterns and rituals, and at determined times through the seasons of the year, appear to be a culmination of such systematic practices in pre-Inca cultures.

Left: The modern Inca Trail near Intipunku, Peru, follows the route of an ancient Inca road from Cuzco.

Above: The modern Plaza de Armas, Cuzco, was the ancient Huacaypata Plaza, centre of the Inca capital.

WHERE ARE THEY NOW?

The Dutch anthropologist Tom Zuidema devoted more than 40 years to the study of *ceques* and the sources of their organization and meaning. The *ceque* routes are described in considerable detail in Cobo's chronicle and other Inca colonial sources. However, the structures, such as towers at *huacas*, have long since been dismantled.

In the late 1970s Zuidema and archaeoastronomer Anthony Aveni devoted four seasons of fieldwork to careful interpretations of the chronicles and surveyed the likely routes of *ceques* and locations of the *huacas* in Cobo's descriptions, using their knowledge of the terrain and landscape around Cuzco. Their efforts proved the validity of the system. In addition to mapping the locations of numerous *huacas*, they located three original places where astronomical *huacas* were used for measurements. One was a pair of towers to mark sunset at the June solstice, situated on a hill called Lacco, north of Cuzco. The second, another pair of towers, marked the December solstice from the Coricancha. The third was four pillars on Cerro Picchu, in western Cuzco, marking planting time; sighted from the *ushnu* stone in the Coricancha, they were used to track the sun on its mid-August passage through its lowest point.

RELIGION AND TRADE

The agricultural staples of Andean civilization were maize corn, the potato and various squashes and legumes. Pastoralism – llama herding – in upland regions and the exploitation of rich marine fauna were practised. In the Andean Area, variety and diversity of crops decreases with altitude. Consequently, people in upland regions were characteristically both farmers and herders because the combination of activities was more productive than either was singly.

In contrast, in lowland areas ancient Andeans tended to be specialists, engaging primarily in agriculture in the coastal desert valleys or in marine fishing. Here, by contrast to the uplands, the pursuit of one activity or the other as a full-time occupation was more productive than practising a combination of the two. In tropical forest areas, people needed to combine several sources of living – farming small cleared forest plots, hunting and fishing the rivers.

EARLY TRADE
Yet, even from the earliest times, although the bulk of the population was engaged in producing food through agriculture or marine fishing, there was contact between different regions for the exchange of the products of different areas. These contrasting activity zones, spaced across the land but with very different farming activities at varying altitudes, required different solutions to the problems of supply and demand, and fostered the classic highland–lowland reciprocal trade of the Andean Area.

In upland regions, communities of farmers tended to be self-sufficient in producing

Left: The importance of maize to northern coastal oasis valley cultures is shown in this Early Intermediate Period effigy vessel of maize cobs.

Above: From the most ancient times, the peoples of valleys and basins used terracing and irrigation channels to maximize land use.

their own essentials through a combination of hill farming and herding. In the lowland valleys and marine fishing areas, however, communities of specialists bartered for each other's produce. The variety of activities for making a living and the practice of exchange between regions naturally led to the movement of people and ideas, as well as of goods, between areas.

The physical nature of water preservation, its distribution in elaborate irrigation systems, the making of raised fields and extensive hill terracing have been described elsewhere. Maximum exploitation was made of physical resources and modifications of the natural landscape to increase production, presumably partly as the solution to rising population. Yet soon, living at mere subsistence level would not be enough for most people.

Above: Inca farmers harvesting a potato crop, depicted by Guaman Poma de Ayala in his Nueva Crónica y Buen Gobierno, c.1613.

GROWTH IN RELIGION

Natural processes were in control of the seasons and thus of the water supply and of agricultural success or failure. Ancient Andeans modified their landscape as much as they could to alleviate the seeming unpredictability of nature. However, lacking scientific explanations for the seasons, their direct observations led to the creation of supernatural explanations, or in other words, religion.

They also began to understand the connections between seasonal changes and recurring natural occurrences in their different regions, for example that drought on the coasts corresponded with greater rainfall in the mountains. All Andeans lived under the same sky, and their observations of the heavens also enabled them to invent explanations for the world around them and to exchange these explanations with each other.

Having moved beyond existing at mere survival level, Andean peoples now related their day-to-day experiences to cosmological ideas that explained them. To appease and solicit the gods who controlled human fate, significant numbers of people in society were devoted to the production of objects that produced no immediate physical subsistence, but did aid spiritual well-being. By the time of the Late Intermediate Period and Late Horizon urban civilizations of the Chimú and the Inca, large numbers of specialist craftspeople were state-sponsored producers of non-essential goods (non-essential only in the sense of not being necessary for survival, but nevertheless considered essential for the well-being of society).

Potters, metallurgists, textile and feather workers were employed by the state to make huge amounts of specialized objects solely for burial and royal tombs. In addition, priests and dedicated royal historians and record-keepers were employed to continue and sustain state religion and history. Furthermore, regional administrators were required to regulate the collection, storage and redistribution of produce to ensure that all citizens of the state had enough to live on, and to support those not actually engaged in agriculture, herding, marine fishing or trading.

TRADE IN RITUAL OBJECTS

For each community to practise its religious beliefs, it needed the objects and images that it perceived to be significant. Finding these items, however, often meant looking outside the settlements, thus expanding trading relationships that had hitherto dealt purely with essential goods.

As urban and ritual sites became more complex and relationships between settlements more elaborate, the exchange of both types of goods grew more organized and sophisticated. The images on pottery, textiles and architecture, and the artefacts found in archaeological sites and burials in the earliest settlements and ritual centres in uplands, lowlands and tropical forests show that each sought the produce and exotic materials of the other.

Marine products such as the thorny oyster, shark teeth, stingray spines and shells were important ritual objects that became essential in ceremony in both upland and lowland religious centres. Likewise, mountain deities, ocean gods and sky gods were considered the explanations or the controllers of human fate. The attributes of tropical animals – particularly jaguars, serpents and monkeys – were revered among mountain and forest dwellers alike. Hallucinogenic products such as mushrooms, coca and cactus buds, essential in shamanism and religious ritual, were traded over great distances.

With trade, direct or indirect, came ideas. Although regions of Andean society worshipped special local deities, there soon developed a core of features that can be called pan-Andean religious concepts.

Below: Coastal valley peoples' reliance on the sea is represented by this Moche stirrup-spout vessel of a fisherman and his totora craft.

COSMOS AND GALAXY

Throughout the world, agricultural societies and others living close to the elements recognized the relationships between the seasons and the cycle of their farming, herding and fishing activities. They also learned to make connections between the movements of the stars and planets and the sequence of their yearly tasks. Ancient Andeans were no exception in this.

We know most about the cosmological beliefs of the Incas in particular because they were partially recorded and preserved by Spanish priests and administrators. General themes through the evolution of Andean civilization show that it is unlikely that Inca beliefs were unique to them, except in certain details. Rather, it seems more likely that Inca cosmology represents, generally, the product of beliefs common throughout the Andean Area. The unusual and specific features of the Andean environment, such as the dramatic mountains, led to responses and explanations that fitted the ancient Andeans' own view of life.

WORLDS ABOVE AND BELOW

Andean cosmology saw the universe as a series of layers. The terrestrial layer – Kai Pacha or Hurin Pacha, the Lower World – is punctuated and represented in numerous sacred places and phenomena called *huacas*, as described earlier. Nature was thought of as a dynamic, living being, composed of interactive forces and perceived in dual and reciprocal form: everything was part male and part female, dark and light, hot and cold, positive and negative. Deep reverence was held for Pacha Mama, the earth mother, and for Viracocha, the creator god (also known by various other names).

Below the terrestrial layer was an inner-terrestrial sphere, Uku Pacha, the World Below, while above was the outer, celestial sphere, Hanan Pacha, the World Above. The underlying primeval belief envisaged a remote past when giant beings and superhumans 'emerged' from the earth to battle for its domination. A great flood then engulfed the world, sweeping away these beings and

Above: The Torréon temple at Machu Picchu was used as an astronomical observatory for sightings of the night sky.

transforming them into the landscape. Thus, they became the mountains and plains, the rivers and valleys, the oceans and rocky shores.

The first humans ascended from Uku Pacha in various versions, coming from caves, from the earth itself and from springs and other earth cavities. Directed by the sky god or creator god, different people chose their homes and occupations in life according to the god's directions. The world before humans became a text of sacred places from the earliest times, representing the story of time and the changing landscape, from super beings to the present human beings. In this way, all life represented a continuous cycle and nourished the reverence for people's

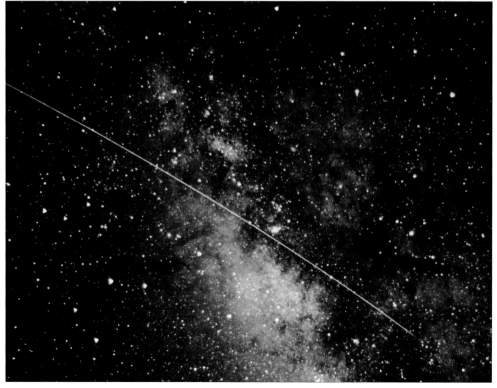

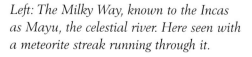

Left: The Milky Way, known to the Incas as Mayu, the celestial river. Here seen with a meteorite streak running through it.

ancestors, who were perceived as beings in another state but still interactive with the present.

CYCLICAL WORLD

These cosmological beliefs fostered a relationship with the earth that strove to work with it rather than to master it. Knowing that elemental forces were beyond their control, and to some extent unpredictable, ancient Andeans believed that there were always balancing forces to maintain the equilibrium over time, and sought the permission of the gods to use the landscape and enjoy its largesse. In this universe, human beings were only one part, and they were considered of less importance than the plants, animals, landscape and celestial bodies who personified the deities.

It was believed that the gods were all-powerful, and could instantly bring about the end of humankind if not worshipped and appeased. Humans could not survive if the sun suddenly ceased to shine, or if the rains stopped for ever.

The world was believed to have evolved and to operate in cycles known as *pachacuti* (literally a 'revolution': from Quechua *cuti*, 'turning over', and *pacha*, 'time and space'). The annual seasons, the revolutions of the stars and planets in the sky, and human life itself were all cyclical, and so incorporated both time and space. The Incas thought of themselves as the final creation in a succession of creations, destructions and re-creations of the world and its inhabitants by the gods in an effort to create the most perfect form of beings to honour them.

THE INCA CALENDAR

Most prominent and observable in Hanan Pacha was Mayu, the Milky Way, the celestial river. Mayu's movements across the night sky were observed keenly by the Incas and their predecessors. Observation of Mayu was the starting point for correlations between the

Above: The Intihuatana (Hitching Post of the Sun), at Qenqo, north of Cuzco, was formed by natural outcrop pillars.

calendar and the natural changes of earthly conditions and seasons. This Andean concept of Mayu as the starting point is in marked contrast to the calculations of most other cultures, which proceed from observations of the movements of the closest single celestial bodies – the sun and the moon. By contrast, their observations of the Milky Way are of a vast galactic rotation.

DIVIDED UNIVERSE

The Incas also partitioned the universe horizontally according to the points of the compass, forming an imaginary cross corresponding to the axis of the Milky Way, which lies between the compass points. This is Mayu's southernmost point of movement in the night sky as it crosses its highest point through a 24-hour period. A vertical axis passed through Hanan Pacha, Hurin Pacha and Uku Pacha, intersecting the centre of the quartered cross and holding the cosmos together as an interacting organic whole.

HEAVENLY CONSTELLATIONS

Observation of the Milky Way as the starting point for formulating a calendar and as the axis of the universe provided an all-encompassing scheme by the Incas to chart the correlations between the positions of the stars and changes on Earth, and to organize daily, seasonal and annual labour and ritual on this basis. The movements of all the celestial bodies were used by the Incas to regulate and predict zoological and botanical cycles, both wild and domestic, and to organize the care of their crops and llama flocks. Theses celestial beings were held responsible for procreation on Earth.

DIVISIONS OF MAYU

The plane of the Milky Way's rotation inclines noticeably from that of the Earth by 26–30 degrees. Mayu's movements follow a sequence that rocks it slowly through the course of the year such that during half the year it tilts from right to left and then changes during the other half of the year to tilt from left to right. When Mayu's movements are plotted from the southern hemisphere, the broad band of the 'river' forms another tripartite division, this time of the sky into three sections: above, below, and Mayu.

These divisions of the sky provided a celestial grid against which all other astronomical observations could be plotted, including not only the obvious luminated planets, stars and constellations but also immense stellar voids, or 'dark cloud' constellations. The Incas devoted considerable effort to tracking and calculating the paths of celestial bodies and constellations. Careful records were kept of the first appearances (heliacal risings) and last settings (heliacal settings) of stars and planets.

DARK MATTERS

Most of the named constellations and prominent individual stars are within or very close to the axial plane of the Milky Way. In Andean astronomy, individual stars or constellations were named as architectural structures or as agricultural implements. Seemingly in contradiction, Andean so-called 'constellations' are the dark spaces, the interstellar dark matter, between the stars.

Above: An Inca astrologer as depicted in Guaman Poma de Ayalaís Nueva Crónica y Buen Gobierno, c.1613, complete with sighting stick and quipu *records.*

To the Incas, these voids were named animal constellations: an adult llama, a baby llama, a fox, a condor, a vulture, a falcon, a tinamou (a partridge-like bird), a toad and a serpent. The luminary bodies included Collca (literally 'the granary'), which is the Pleiades; Orqoi-Cilay (literally 'the multicoloured llama'), another star group, and Chaska-Qoylor (literally 'the shaggy star'), which is also known as Venus or the morning 'star'.

CONSTELLATIONS AND MYTHS

Practical observations and applications were interwoven with myth. For example, the toad constellation, although he creeps across the night sky, always wins the nocturnal race against the tinamou, for the tinamou, or *yutu*, is slow and stupid and flies around aimlessly when stirred.

Left: The dark spaces between the stars represented various constellations to the Incas, including the condor and the fox.

Right: The Horca del Inca, Bolivia, is one of many ridge-line sets of stone pillars for astronomical sightings.

The solstices of Mayu coincide with the Andean wet and dry seasons, and thus the celestial river was used to predict seasonal water cycles. Yacana, the 'dark cloud' llama disappears at midnight, when it was believed to have descended to Earth to drink water and thus prevent flooding. In contrast, black llamas were starved during October, in the dry season, in order to make them weep, seen as a supplication to the gods for rain.

Collca, the Pleiades, disappears from the night sky in mid-April, at the beginning of harvest. It reappears in the sky in early June, after the harvest has been gathered, and is thus associated throughout the Andes with these activities and called 'The Storehouse'.

One *ceque* route from Cuzco also associates myth with the Pleiades. A female coronation gift made from a provincial chief to Huáscar was Cori Qoyllur, 'Golden Star'. She proceeded along the *ceque*, stopping at *huacas* on the route for banquets and to make sacrificial offerings to the gods. The *ceque* itself is aligned with the disappearance of the Pleiades in mid-April. Another *huaca* marks the sun's lowest point on 18 August, the beginning of maize-sowing. Cori Qoyllur thus represents wives who walk the *ceque* at night and are transformed into *huaca* stones. Cori Qoyllur was herself turned to stone as a *huaca*, marking the point where the Pleiades disappear, and she is held responsible for fecundity in the Inca universe.

CELESTIAL MOVEMENTS

The movements of the sun were used to calculate the two most important ritual dates in the year – the winter and summer solstices, Capac Raymi and Inti Raymi.

In like manner, the first appearance of the Pleiades just before sunrise was correlated with the regular sidereal lunar months (the 27.3-day period of the rotation of the moon around the Earth– moon centre of mass), beginning on 8–9 June and ending on 3–4 May. In Ayrihua (the month of April), as this lunar-plotted year ended, there were ceremonies in Cuzco honouring the royal insignia, and a pure white llama was dressed in a red tunic and fed coca (*Erythroxylon coca*) and *chicha* (maize beer) to symbolize the first llama to appear on Earth after the great flood that destroyed the previous world.

AXIS OF THE MILKY WAY

Mayu's movements were reflected in the organization of the Inca Empire into its four quarters, and also regulated the routes of the four principal highways emanating from Cuzco to these quarters. For, except for a certain necessity to respect the physical demands of the landscape, these routes approximated the axis of the Milky Way, which lies between the compass points. Mayu's axes were also associated with sacred *ceque* ritual alignments, at least one of which correlated to the southernmost point in the Milky Way's movements.

EARLY SETTLERS TO EMPIRE BUILDERS

The sweep of human history in the New World started at least 15,000 years ago, when humans migrated into the New World from the Old World, though the exact timing and detail of how long this journey took are obscured in the distant past.

During the Lithic, or Archaic, Period, humans began to live a more sedentary lifestyle. As with early human culture in the Old World, the existence and nature of the beliefs of these earliest South Americans can only be deduced from the very few facts available, combined with speculation.

In the earliest settlements, South Americans developed a more stable source of food in the beginnings of domestication of both plants and animals. Hunting and gathering and the exploitation of sea resources were never abandoned, however.

Later, the development of ceramics and, later still, metallurgy brought greater and greater divisions of labour within Andean societies, and consequently greater complexity. Sophisticated architecture, including U-shaped complexes, and masonry and adobe building techniques also developed.

Social hierarchies, elitism and rulership evolved alongside technological advances, as did religious belief and the explanation of human existence. In the absence of written records, archaeologists and historians seeking to understand the nature of the earliest Andean societies can only project what they know of later societies into the past.

Left: A marching, club-wielding warrior of the procession carved on stone monoliths at Cerro Sechin.

THE FIRST ARRIVALS

The story of the human colonization of the North and South American continents began at least 15,000 years ago. The earliest dating for human occupation comes from Monte Verde, southern Chile – about 14,850 years ago. Following herds of migratory land animals, and possibly sea animals as well, intrepid colonizers, the Palaeo-Indians, crossed the Bering Strait when world climatic change created a land bridge there at the end of the last great glacial period.

The new continent was occupied by an abundance of fauna and flora, most of which had evolved indigenously, independent of Old World animals and plants, for millions of years. Some of the large game animals or their immediate ancestors, such as the Columbian mammoth, or American mastodon, had probably migrated from Asia during earlier breaks, known as interstadials, in world glacial periods long before the human migration, when climatic fluctuations had opened and closed earlier Bering land bridges.

The Lithic culture of this period persisted for about 10,000 years, to about 5,000 years ago, when post-Ice Age (Pleistocene) sea

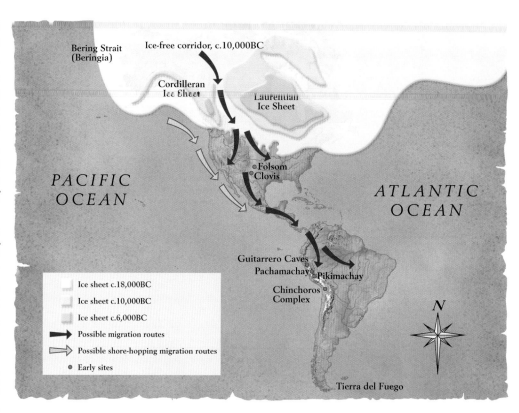

Above: Map of the early settlements of South America showing possible migration routes and the shrinking of the ice sheet.

Below: Migrants used stemmed chert spear points with the atl-atl (spear thrower).

levels became stable at about where they are today. During this time definitive changes occurred in climate and environment: glaciers retreated from huge sheets of ice to mountain isolation; global ocean levels rose by about 100m (330ft); ecological zones shifted as climate changed and animals, plants and humans migrated to higher altitudes; meteorological patterns and marine currents shifted. The results were the climatic and environmental conditions of the present.

MIGRATION ROUTES

Evidence for the very earliest human occupants in North America is sparse. Only the records for the later millennia of the Lithic Period are more abundant. Several claims for much earlier human occupation, from several sites in South America – for example Pikimachay Cave, Peru, 20,000 years ago – are not universally accepted. Nevertheless, the long journey from northernmost North America into and throughout South America must have taken place over many generations, indicating that migration probably began significantly earlier than the earliest dates for occupation in Chile.

The geologically traced pattern of glaciation in North America reveals an ice-free corridor between the great glacial sheets of Canada, through mid-continent, at this migration period. It has long been assumed that this was the most logical route into the interior. It has also been argued that an equally viable route would have been along the western coasts. Any evidence for coastal migration, if it exists, lies beneath the present ocean. Nevertheless, radiocarbon dates from Peruvian and Chilean coastal sites prove that occupation along the shoreline began at least 11,500 years ago, from the time when evidence for occupation in the New World in general is more abundant. Another recent theory suggests that a smaller and earlier migration possibly

Above: Large, fluted spear points, such as this chert Palaeo-Indian Folsom point, were used to hunt big game.

came from Europe across the ice floes of the North Atlantic into north-eastern North America. This argument is based on conclusions about similarities between the Solutrian lithic culture of south-western France, which flourished about 22,000 to 16,500 years ago, and the Clovis stone point tradition of North America, though this theory is rigorously disputed.

PALAEO-INDIAN SITES

The pace of migration is impossible to calculate and can be based only on a set of assumptions and speculations about population numbers, available game and other living resources, and the need to continue moving south. Thus, the precise time of the beginning and the exact nature of the migration cannot be known.

The evidence of molecular biology and DNA in contemporary Native Americans proves descent from three or four biologically distinct populations. There were, therefore, several incidents of original migration by different groups into North America. The biology and blood-group evidence shows that descendants from only one of these groups crossed the Isthmus of Panama into South America.

The earliest confirmed, substantially occupied Palaeo-Indian site is Monte Verde, Chile. Here were found round sling stones, grooved stones for use in a bolas, and chipped stone artefacts, including long projectile points, scrapers mounted on wooden handles and possibly a drill. Other wooden finds include a lance, digging sticks and mortars. Dwelling remains were of pole-and-animal-skin-framed huts, joined at their sides and forming two rows. Separate was an isolated, open-sided, wishbone-shaped structure with a small platform at the back. Its packed sand and gravel floor had remains of burnt medicinal plants and chewed leaves, and around the structure were hearths, medicinal plants and mastodon bones.

Other Palaeo-Indian sites with several traditions of fluted projectile-point shapes, including harpoon points for maritime hunting, have been found; they generally date from about 11,500 years ago and later.

PLANTS AND BELIEFS

The earliest-known domesticated plants come from this early period, from Guitarrero Cave, northern Peru. Although fibre plants dominated the findings, specimens of domesticated beans and chilli peppers were found, both *not* native to the region and thus cultivated there.

Representations of the earliest Andean beliefs are partly actual and partly speculative. There are suggestions of some form of shamanism and perhaps a belief in a multi-layered world with the Earth layered between celestial and inner spheres. The remains at Monte Verde show special use of plants and animal bones at a specialized structure, supporting shamanism. Concrete evidence of belief in an afterlife, or at least the honouring of selected deceased, comes from fishing settlements at Chinchorros and La Paloma on the central Peruvian coast. From the former come the earliest mummified remains in Andean culture (*c.*5000BC). From the latter come the first bodies buried in an articulated, decorated state.

Below: The coastal peoples of the Chinchorros culture (c.6000–1600BC) mummified chosen individuals after death.

DEVELOPING COMMUNITIES

The Lithic Period did not end abruptly. An increasingly sedentary lifestyle developed towards the end of the period in some areas of South America, while in others a hunter-gatherer economy continued to form most or a significant part of people's lifestyles. In the Andean Area, village life became more important as an adaptation to developments in climate and habitat in the post-Ice Age environment. Sedentism, or the shift of people from living in non-permanent settlements to permanent settlements, was not at first accompanied by the development of pot-making in Andean South America, and so archaeologists call the period the Preceramic, or Formative, Period, or sometimes the Cotton Preceramic.

EARLY DOMESTICATION

Recognition of the usefulness of particular plants and animals fostered the special observation of these species and gradual greater attendance to their care and proliferation. The process of domestication was an evolutionary one, helped wittingly by humans but with practical rather than specific scientific understanding. In the archaeological record, the end result is recognizable only when genetic changes render the plants and animals biologically distinguishable from their wild progenitors. Thus, the beginning of the process cannot be pinpointed in time.

The results, however, show anatomical changes that are unmistakable. Equally, the regular cultivation of species in areas outside their normal wild distributions shows human mastery over their use. The earliest known domesticated plants date to about 10,000 years ago in the Andean Area, from Guitarrero Cave in northern Peru. Fibre plants dominate most assemblages of Lithic Period sites. Numerous wild hemp-like plants were used to make a wide range of artefacts, from tools and clothing to bedding. Many other kinds of plant were apparently of medicinal importance – and perhaps also of religious importance.

At Guitarrero Cave, locally native tubers, rhizomes, fruits, chillies and beans were found; from Tres Ventanas Cave, central Peru, at an altitude of 3,900m (12,800ft), also come tubers – ulluco and the potato; and from several cave deposits in the Ayacucho region come gourds.

THE FIRST CIVILIZATION?

As sedentary lifestyles increased from the time of these earliest domesticated plants to about 5,000 years ago, communities derived greater proportions of their nutrition from this source, alongside intensive tending and gathering of wild food sources. Andean Preceramic communities cultivated mostly self-watering regions, relying on rainfall and river run-off, and developed agro-pastoralism with llama herding. Coastal peoples pursued lifestyles exploiting the rich marine resources and cultivated cotton in seasonally watered valley bottoms. Such diversity was the beginning of the highland–lowland (or coastal) division.

The variety of environments within the Andean Area, both in different regions and at different heights, discouraged integration between communities, although it was forged within them. Nevertheless, the products of different regions were sought after and traded over long distances with increasing regularity, and with this trade the exchange of ideas was inevitable.

There is little evidence for powerful regional political leadership, but there *is* evidence of integrated communal effort in the form of the first monumental architecture between about 3000 and 2000BC. Inter-regional contact and trade also began the long Andean tradition of textile use – cotton cultivated in the lowlands and llama wool from herding in the highlands continued the earlier Andean Area focus on fibre technology, including the earliest weaving.

ARCHITECTURE AND TEXTILES

Increasing reliance on cultivation drew sierra populations to lower altitudes, into well-watered highland valleys and basins. Shared religious beliefs, manifested in architecture and on textiles, is known as

Left: The Preceramic Period adobe mud sculpture at the Temple of the Crossed Hands, at Kotosh (c.3000BC).

the Kotosh Religious Tradition in the highlands, after Kotosh, a site in highland central Peru at about 2,000m (6,600ft). Farther north, La Galgada was another highland valley community. Along the western coast more than a score of early sites are known, including Huaca Prieta, Salinas de Chao, Aspero and El Paraíso in north-central coastal Peru. Here architectural traditions called Supe, Aspero and El Paraíso developed.

The architecture at these sites varies in detail. For example, Supe Tradition communal structures are smaller and are associated with domestic buildings and artefacts, indicating they were constructed by their local communities. The much larger structures at sites of other traditions indicate more regional communal efforts, as centres for several communities. What is common, however, is the beginning of Andean central worship and a long generic tradition of ceremonial mounds and sunken courts or plazas. Both oval and rectangular examples

Below: Cotton, domesticated by at least 3000BC in the northern Peruvian coastal valleys, was a valuable commodity to trade.

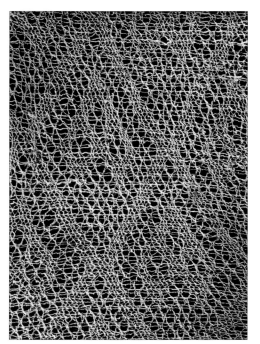

of sunken plazas are known. The two elements were made adjacent to each other and, in general, the plazas were smaller in area than the adjacent mounds.

These combined civic-ceremonial constructions are the earliest manifestations of Andean universal belief. They show both vertical and horizontal divisions of space for ceremonial purposes, and the special making and use of such space for communal worship drawing several communities together.

Alongside these architectural developments, textile design and decoration began to predominate among other media, such as stone, bone, shell, gourds, wood and basketry. Cotton was twined with spaced wefts and exposed warps; looping, knotting and simple weaving were also developed. The geometric nature of lattice-like fabric lent itself to

Above: Cotton was typically woven into open-work fabrics, such as this Chancay textile from the Late Intermediate Period.

angular decoration in different colours and to symmetry. Stripes, diamonds, squares and chevrons were used individually, in patterns, and to depict humanlike beings and animals that were important locally in an economic sense and universally as revered beings. Crabs, fish, raptors and serpents predominate.

Although the specifics of belief systems of such an early period can only be surmised, such detailed imagery, through its universality and repetition, reveals underlying religious belief. Coastal animals and motifs were copied in the highland traditions and vice versa. It seems that religion was, even at this early period, at the foundations of Andean civilization.

NEW AGRICULTURE AND ARCHITECTURE

The environmental diversity within the Andean Area meant that communities had to adapt in varying ways to suit conditions. The increasingly sedentary lifestyles of ancient Andeans reveals their increasing ability to manipulate the environment to increase domesticated production. However, progress was uneven. The wild progenitors of the classic cultigens that provided the bulk of carbohydrate and protein nutrition of ancient Andeans – maize, potatoes, beans and squashes – were native to different altitudes and regions, as were llamas and the other camelid species.

Following the Preceramic Period, the pre-eminent technological developments were pottery and irrigation agriculture. Archaeologists call it the Initial Period.

FARMING AND CERAMICS

In South America, pottery-making was discovered outside the Andean Area. The earliest ceramics were made in coastal Ecuador by the end of the 6th millennium BC, and the well-watered tropical areas of Colombia and Ecuador were the first areas where the 'civilization-defining' combination of intensive agriculture and pot-making became the predominant lifestyle by about 3000BC. The spread of intensive farming and ceramics followed a path of least resistance, from low self-watered environments to higher self-watered regions, to the more arid high Andes and western coasts.

By about 1800BC the combination was well established in northern and central highland Peru and in the fertile valleys of the north-central coast; by 1600BC, communities in the Titicaca Basin in the southern Andes were making pottery; and another few hundred years later ceramics had diffused to the dry coasts of southern Peru and northern Chile. In Altiplano regions, however, agriculture was combined with llama herding, while in coastal valleys agriculture was teamed with fishing.

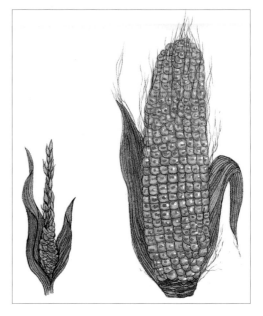

*Above: From its diminutive wild ancestor, maize (*Zea mays*) spread into the Andean Area from Mesoamerica.*

PAN-ANDEAN FOUNDATIONS

The increased security of grown food and rich sea resources, together with plentiful supplies of cotton and wool, made increases in population inevitable. With the ability to irrigate and terrace the valleys and basins and thereby increase the yields and available land for agriculture, new areas could be opened. The practice of exchange of coastal and highland products continued the flow of contact among otherwise independent regions and communities. At the same time, the architectural and religious practices begun in Preceramic days continued.

The intensified concern with stable agriculture deepened the reverence for 'mother earth', setting the stage for the veneration of Pacha Mama (as she was known to the Inca). The need to regulate agricultural, herding and fishing activities throughout the year encouraged careful observation of heavenly bodies, the stars

Left: The people of Garagay decorated their ceremonial centres with sculpted and painted adobe walls.

Above: Garagay in the Rimac-Chillon Valley, central Peru, was a typical coastal U-shaped civic-ceremonial centre in the Initial Period.

and constellations, and of Mayu (the Milky Way) as a whole. These two facets were the fundamental elements of ancient Andean religion. The strengthening and consolidation of these foundations in the Initial Period secured their prevalence throughout the remainder of Andean ancient history.

U-SHAPED COMPLEXES
The Preceramic Period tradition of monumental architecture continued. It was a great age of civic-ceremonial construction. Hundreds of sites are known but relatively few have been excavated extensively.

Ceremonial mounds and platforms were built up using soil-filled mesh bags for interior bulk and adobe brick exteriors. Clearing the silt that built up in irrigation canals provided an abundance of suitable fine clays for bricks to build bigger and more elaborate structures. Sunken courts became larger, presumably to accommodate growing congregations. Subterranean temple complexes became more extensive and façades were decorated with relief sculpture and painted in bright colours.

The Paraíso Tradition that started in the Preceramic Period developed the enduring form of civic-ceremonial architecture in the northern Andean Area – the U-shaped complex. Regional details varied, as ever, but the classic elements were the same everywhere. A large central platform-mound formed the base of the U. In front of it, flanking a large central plaza, were two lower, elongated platforms. Variations included rectangular or circular sunken courts, wings extending from the central platform, walled vestibules and multiple temples on the platforms.

The builders of ancient ceremonial complexes seemed consciously to vie with one another in ostentation and display. Visual impact was important. Themes for enduring Andean architectural religious advertisement are exemplified by Cerro Sechín, where at least 27 megalithic slabs were erected along the front of the temple mound, carved in low relief. They depict dead individuals, many of them dismembered, and individual heads in a gruesome afterlife procession. At Garagay and Moxeke, human–animal transformation is depicted in adobe friezes of insects with human heads, fanged heads in spider webs, humans with

fangs and condor features. At Huaca de los Reyes there is an adobe head sculpture with a fanged mouth.

The largest U-shaped complexes were in the coastal valleys: Sechín Alto, Sechín Bajo, Cerro Sechín, Huaca de los Reyes, El Paraíso, Cardal, Garagay, La Florida and Moxeke-Pampa de los Llamas. A prominent highland example is La Galgada.

In the Titicaca Basin, a separate architectural tradition began at Chiripa, featuring a large mound with a central sunken court at the top surrounded by rectangular temples.

EXPANSION HALTED
Communal practices of civic-ceremonial construction begun in Preceramic times increased with the communal activities of canal building and shared land use. The intensification of farming, herding and fishing, expansion into new areas and increased growth to support a great labour force were self-propelling processes. Their only limitations were the availability of land and the unpredictabililty of climate.

And so it was. For beginning about 900BC, towards the end of the Initial Period, the pattern of El Niño and related climatic events brought severe drought that prevailed for centuries.

ORACLE AND SHRINE: CHAVÍN DE HUÁNTAR

Generalized themes permeated Andean cultures during the Initial Period. Although the valleys, mountain basins and coastal oases were largely independent, each was dominated by one or a few civic-ceremonial centres, and religion was developing across communities as a unifying theme. This process culminated in the first great period of region-wide unification: the Early Horizon.

DROUGHT AND DISASTER

The prolonged drought that began and defined the end of the Initial Period was a phenomenon not previously experienced by Andean farmers. Disaster ensued as crops failed year upon year. The new irrigation systems could not cope, and the extra land brought into cultivation as village farming became more efficient and sophisticated was useless when drought prevented farmers from watering it.

Before they abandoned many of the sites, the ancient builders of the U-shaped civic-ceremonial complexes must have devoted considerable time in pondering why the gods had forsaken them.

Below: The mysterious Lanzón Stone was erected in the dark oracular chamber within the Old Temple at Chavín de Huántar.

Above: Sharp-toothed images of stylized caymans were a common symbolic Chavín motif in stone carvings on walls.

A UNIFYING CENTRE

The regularity and the quantity of rainfall began to increase again from about 800BC. By now, northern sierra and coastal Andean communities that had weathered the drought through several generations were very subdued. However, religious themes that had begun in the Initial Period did not disappear; instead they re-emerged within two extensive regional spheres of influence – the northern and southern Andean Area – under the newly encouraging conditions.

The more widespread unifying sphere was centred in the northern Andean Area at Chavín de Huántar, sited on the eastern slopes of the Cordillera Blanca in the Mosna Valley, more than 3,000m (9,800ft) above sea level.

Chavín de Huántar was established about 900BC or shortly after, at the beginning of the drought, as a new U-shaped civic-ceremonial centre joining La Galgada as an extension of the U-shaped Tradition that had developed in the coastal valleys. It went through several phases of development, initially mainly confined within its immediate valley as it persisted through the drought years. Chavín de Huántar appears to have been deliberately and strategically located in the Andes

roughly midway between the coast to the west and the tropical lowlands to the east. From its position it controlled several passes running between mountains. In a time of scarcity, but with an entrenched tradition of inter-regional exchange, such a strategic position must have given Chavín special status and importance among declining civic-ceremonial sites. Its location appears to cater to both the mountain deities, believed to control the weather and rainfall, and the coastal deities, where the revered Pacha Mama (earth mother) of valleys that were once productive was apparently now forsaking her people.

As climatic conditions and agricultural production improved, Chavín's artistic influence began to spread. With its distinctive symbolic art, it became the source and focus of a pan-Andean religion. Principal themes focused on feline and serpentine attributes, on fish and other aquatic animals, on human-like raptors, and on a pervasive Staff Deity. These images appeared on the architecture of Chavín de Huántar itself, and on Chavín

Below: Tenoned, stone severed heads, with feline canines, were typical wall 'decorations' at Chavín de Huántar.

Above: The façade of the New Temple at Chavín de Huántar, which incorporated and enlarged the Old Temple from c.500BC.

ceramics, textiles and metalwork. The spread of Chavín symbolic art went hand-in-hand with its equally crucial role in the spreading of emerging technology.

BIRTH OF A CULT

Chavín was not the largest ceremonial centre of the Early Horizon, but it was certainly one of the most elaborate. It does not seem to have been a centre of political power or unity, except perhaps within its valley, but it was a unifying centre for religions. Although not truly urban in layout and proportions, it must have accommodated a resident population of priests, officials, artisans, servants and pilgrims to support and serve the cult. Its deliberate establishment at the beginning of the drought period and persistence through it must have made it seem a particularly blessed ceremonial centre to ancient Andeans. It therefore became the focus of pilgrimage for peoples throughout the northern Andes.

The centre of the site was a classic U-shaped complex, which went through several phases of temple development, both inside and out. Within its base ceremonial platform, called the Castillo, was a multi-galleried temple. The original (Old) temple housed the cult object of the Lanzón, an obelisk-like, lance-shaped stone

carved with human, feline and serpent attributes and the snarling mouth of the Chavín supreme deity. The gallery holding it has an upper oracular chamber.

The New Temple, which combined and enlarged the Old, was entered through an elaborate doorway: the Black and White Portal. Its two columns – dark (male) and light (female) – were carved with human-like raptor figures. The New Temple housed the cult figure known as the Raimundi Stela, an elaborately carved slab depicting the Staff Deity.

In the courtyard outside the temple complex stood the Tello Obelisk, a huge stone carved with two jungle caymans, and other animal and plant symbols.

The temple galleries included an elaborate system of water channels. When water was flushed through the system, accompanying acoustic properties literally made the temple roar.

Chavín's importance lasted for some 700 years, into the 3rd century BC. The power of its cult continued to spread through a second period of drought, roughly 400–200BC, the persistence of which perhaps precipitated its eventual decline.

STAFF DEITY AND TROPHY HEADS

One of the most prominent Chavín deities was the Staff Deity. This was a figure with feline, raptor and serpentine attributes, holding a staff in each hand with outstretched arms on either side of the body. Sometimes the staves were serpents. The Staff Deity could be male or female, identifiable by distinctive characteristics.

Another distinctive Chavín Cult theme was the trophy head. Appearing on all media, these were disembodied human heads, often with feline or serpentine attributes, thought to portray shamanistic transformation.

Below: The dual-columned stone Black and White Portal of the New Temple at Chavín de Huántar.

SOUTHERN CULTS: PARACAS AND PUKARÁ

Environmental decline occurred in the southern Andean Area, along the coast and in the Altiplano in the late Initial Period. In the Peruvian southern coastal desert, the natural aridity, exacerbated by drought in the inland mountains, presented a considerable challenge to the ingenuity of the coastal fishing village inhabitants. In the Titicaca Basin, the lake level fell dramatically and fields were abandoned all along the southern shores, as farmers could no longer raise crops or feed animals there.

PARACAS MUMMY BURIALS

The Paracas Peninsula was the site of a necropolis of elite burials. Apart from the Chinchorros mummy burials in northern Chile, the Paracas desiccated mummies are the earliest in the Andean Area, beginning a long tradition of mummification in Andean civilization. The elaborately wrapped, multilayered burial bundles demonstrate a preoccupation with the continued life, or participation in the present, of physically deceased important individuals. The richest ceramic and textile products, and exotic goods from afar, were saved for the burials; indeed, some goods were produced specifically for this purpose. Their existence begins the equally long Andean tradition of ancestor worship.

While the peninsula is the site of the Cavernas cemetery, the inhabitants who created it lived in the adjacent area inland around Cerro Colorado, where some 54ha (137 acres) of scattered domestic architecture has been found. The economy was based on local fishing.

The cemetery was a specially dedicated site. The dead were placed in their mummy bundles into large subterranean crypts, which were either bell-shaped pits or masonry-lined rectangular mausoleums. These were used through several generations, and the individuals appear to be kin. As the numbers of burials appear to exceed the requirements of the immediate adjacent settlements, it is

Above: The flying Oculate Being of the Paracas and Nazca southern coastal cultures, depicted on a woollen burial shroud.

thought that the necropolis was also a pilgrimage or cult centre serving communities through a wider region.

The stages for the preparation for these burials were inland in the Chincha Valley. These comprised low rectangular mounds aligned at the front and back of a high-walled central court, sunk to near ground level, such as the one found at Huaca Soto. The court walls are so thick that the complex is reminiscent of a single mound with a sunken summit courtyard. Huaca Soto comprised two interior courts, plus a thick-walled frontal entry court. The whole structure was 70m (230ft) by 200m (650ft) and stood 15m (49) high.

IMPORTANCE OF PUKARÁ

In the Altiplano around Lake Titicaca, emphasis on mother earth (Pacha Mama) and father sky (Yama Mama) continued as people remained close to the land and struggled to cope with drought. The importance of the regional centre at Chiripa waned and the site was eventually left to decline. The replacement for Chiripa as the focus of religion became the ceremonial centre of Pukará, some 75km (47 miles) north-west of the lake. Pukará arose around 400BC and exerted its influence over the Titicaca Basin for four centuries.

Unlike U-shaped complexes, Pukará comprised monumental masonry-clad structures terraced against the hillside. The principal terrace had a monumental staircase and was topped by a rectangular sunken court with one-room buildings around three sides, reminiscent of the Chiripa complex.

The hallmark of Pukará cult symbolic art was the depiction of *yaya* (male) and *mama* (female) figures on opposite sides of slab monoliths erected at Pukará and other sites. Other Pukará stone carving, pottery and textiles displayed ubiquitous Andean images, including felines, serpents, lizards and fish.

Like the Chavín Cult, Pukará art images featured disembodied human heads. Some of these were trophy heads accompanying realistically depicted humans; others accompanied supernatural beings with feline or serpentine attributes, as in the Chavín Cult, and are thought to represent shamans in transformational states. Many Pukará temple sites were rebuilt and used over several centuries. The assemblages of structures around Pukará sunken courts show considerable variety.

Above: Nested geometric patterns in the Pukará culture included the multi-stepped 'Andean Cross'.

In this way, Paracas, Pukará and Chavín styles, although distinct, show themselves to have a pan-Andean combination of features, including, especially, the Chavín emphasis on feline, serpentine and raptor attributes. The combination of cotton textiles and the importation of alpaca and llama wool for use by Paracas weavers shows another highland influence.

THE OCULATE BEING

One supernatural being or deity that stands out as distinctly Paracas, and which carries on in the succeeding Nazca civilization, is known as the Oculate Being. Depicted on textiles, the being was portrayed horizontally – as if flying upside-down – as if looking down on humankind, and crouching. His/her frontal face has characteristic large, circular, staring eyes, and long, streaming appendages originate from various parts of the body and end in trophy heads or small figures.

Below: The bodies of Paracas mummies were tightly constricted into compact bundles and held by cords.

Below: Early Horizon Paracas mummified bodies were buried in multiple layers of cloth, the richness of which reflected their status.

PARACAS AND PUKARÁ LINKS

There are generic artistic links between the Paracas and Pukará art styles and symbols used. Both styles feature monochrome and polychrome pottery with multicoloured motifs framed with incised lines. Some of the earliest phase styles, especially at Paracas, are attributed to Chavín influence because they represent a change from the local pottery that preceded it. There is an emphasis on non-human faces adorned with fangs and feline whiskers, especially on pottery. As Paracas pottery developed, it showed a more naturalistic style akin to Pukará ceramics. Local coastal subjects such as falcons, swallows, owls and foxes later predominated. The images and patterns painted on Paracas pottery were also used in their textiles.

NAZCA CONFEDERACY AND MOCHE STATE

Cult foci such as Chavín, Paracas and Pukará represent distinct local political entities that were united between their regions predominantly by religion. The following Early Intermediate Period saw the break up of Chavín's religious unity, but also the rise of at least one regional state political unity.

COASTAL POWER BASES

As in the Early Horizon, there were two principal regional bases: one north, one south – both coast-based. Centres between mountains and on the Altiplano persisted, but by about 200BC Chavín de Huántar had begun to wane and its importance as a pilgrimage centre was languishing. The construction of new monumental architecture became restrained in central and northern Peruvian valleys that lay between mountains. The decline of Chavín influence is attributed to it lacking the political attributes necessary to maintain long-term stability.

Below: Exposed Nazca group burial in the southern coastal desert. Tombs were often reopened to insert new mummy bundles.

In the Titicaca Basin, Pukará was eclipsed by its contemporary and power inheritor, Tiwanaku. The real political ascendancy of Tiwanaku in the southern Altiplano, however, was yet to dominate the region, although the monumental architecture that was to become its hallmark had begun.

A NEW CULT CENTRE

Nazca civilization flourished in the southern Peruvian coast and adjacent inland valleys from c.100BC to c.AD700. It continued the Andean tradition of religious cult practices by remaining a focus of regional worship and pilgrimage.

The dominance of daily life by ritual was emphasized across the desert floor by the Nazca geoglyphs, whose nature and importance in ritual have been described earlier. Perhaps like the Paracas necropolis, the sheer number of lines and ritual pathways, and the apparent short-term use of many of them, meant that they served a much wider community than just the settlements immediately nearest them.

Above: Nazca woven and dyed woollen tunic, exemplifying the exchange of highland llama wool for coastal craftsmanship.

THE NAZCA CONFEDERACY

Two of the most important Nazca settlements were Cahuachi and Ventilla, the first a ritual 'city', the second an urban 'capital'. Ventilla, the largest Nazca site recorded, covered at least 200ha (495 acres) with terraced housing, walled courts and mounds. It was linked to its ceremonial and ritual counterpart by a Nazca line across the desert.

Through the centuries, increasing drought in the highlands to the east caused growing aridity in the coastal plains. Such was the pressure for water that the Nazca invented an ingenious system of underground aqueducts and galleries to collect and channel underground waters around Cahuachi to minimize evaporation and to provide water in the dry season.

On pottery and textiles the Nazca continued to develop themes begun by people in the Paracas culture. Preoccupied

Above: The strong facial features on this Moche effigy-jar indicate it may have been a portrait of a real person, who seems to be male.

with and motivated by religious symbolic art and ceremonial ritual, they used mythical beings and deities to decorate effigy vessels and cloth with serpent beings, monkeys and other animals, and trophy heads. A cult practice collected caches of trepanned, severed trophy skulls of sacrificial victims in Nazca cemeteries.

Nazca settlements appear to be in part a continuation of Paracas, since Paracas layers are found beneath some Nazca settlements. The cooperative nature of Nazca culture for control of water and for making geoglyphs shows strong ties with other regions but no centralized political power. It was more like a confederate state of independent but highly interacting cities.

THE MOCHE STATE
In the northern Peruvian coastal valleys, the roughly contemporary Moche created the Andean Area's first true state. Here a Moche elite embarked on military domination of the northern valleys between the Sechura Desert and the Casma Valley. They ruled from their capital at Cerro Blanco in the Moche Valley, where by AD450 two huge pyramidal structures of adobe bricks had become the focus of political and religious power. The Huaca del Sol was a four-tiered, cross-shaped platform with a ramp on the north side; the Huaca de la Luna, at the foot of Cerro Blanco, was a three-tiered structure with walls that were richly decorated by friezes depicting mythological scenes and deities. The two ceremonial platforms sat within a sprawling metropolis, which at its maximum size occupied about 3 sq km (740 acres).

Roughly 100 years later, a sand sheet choked the canal system and stifled agriculture, causing abandonment. The focus of Moche politics and religion shifted north to the Lambayeque Valley, to the sites of Pampa Grande and Sipán. The rise of the Wari State, to the south-east out of the Andes, also appears to have been an influence.

The large city of Pampa Grande covered some 6 sq km (1,485 acres) and flourished for about 150 years. Its most imposing structure, Huaca Fortaleza, had a similar function to Huaca del Sol and was the focus of the elite residents of the city. Like Cerro Blanco, Pampa Grande was abandoned abruptly, owing to a combination of agricultural disaster caused by an El Niño weather event and the continued expansion of the Wari State. Internal unrest may also have been a factor.

Left: A pattern of crabs sculpted in adobe mud on a wall frieze at the Huaca de la Luna, Moche, shows its coastal heritage.

Above: In all Pacific coastal cultures, seafood formed an important part of the local cuisine, such as this crayfish on a Nazca pot.

A DERIVED CULT
Moche imagery became a potent religion, with distinctive art symbols and a pantheon of gods much derived from the Chavín Cult. It was characterized by humans and humanized animal figures, serpents, frogs, birds (owls in particular) and sea animals (crabs and fishes), and by standardized groups and ceremonial scenes, including a coca ritual recognizable by distinctive clothing and ritual combat.

Murals, friezes and decorative designs on pottery depict the capture and sacrifice of 'enemies', drinks offered by subordinates to lords and gods, and persons passing through the night sky in moon-shaped boats. Richly furnished burials at Sipán, which are some of the few unlooted tombs of the Andes, reflect scenes that confirm the images on walls, ceramics, textiles and metalwork excavated from other Moche sites.

Although the names of the Moche deities ae not known, the later Chimú Ai Apaec and Si (sky/creator god and moon goddess) may have derived from Moche deities. Especially prominent on ceramics and textiles is the ritual depiction and rich ceremony of the Decapitator God. A Moche mountain god has been identified in an oft-depicted feline-featured being.

MOUNTAIN EMPIRES: WARI AND TIWANAKU

In the Middle Horizon, ancient Andeans began to consolidate large areas of land into political states for the first time. Politics and religion became a corporate whole in official state cults that were imposed with military and economic conquest. Local religious deities were assimilated, easing the imposition of official state religion.

Two dominating empires arose: Wari in the north and Tiwanaku in the south. Despite political and military rivalry, both cultures shared a use of religious iconography and symbols, which arose as a result of their collection and consolidation of the local deities, cults and similarities in religious imagery in the regions they conquered.

Below: Sculptured stone severed heads are tenoned into the walls of the Kalasasaya sunken court at Tiwanku.

DOMINATING THE HIGHLANDS
The city of Huari, which had been established in the preceding Early Intermediate Period, began rapid expansion within the central Andean Huamanga and Huanta basins from about AD600. For the next 200 years its armies conquered and dominated the highlands and coastal valleys of central and northern Peru almost to the present Ecuadorian border.

The capital city occupied a plateau among mountains, 2,800m (9,200ft) above sea level. As a civic, residential and religious centre, it grew rapidly to cover more than 300ha (740 acres), with peripheral residential suburbs occupying a further 250ha (620 acres). Alongside military expansion, the Wari spread a religious hegemony characterized by a distinctive use of symbolic art, much of which shows continuity with ancient Chavín traditions, which survived the political fragmentation of the Early Intermediate Period. Shortly before AD800, however, a political crisis caused building within the capital to abate rapidly and cease. At the same time, Pachacamac, a political centre and religious shrine on the central Peruvian coast that had flourished as a cult centre since the later Early Intermediate Period, and which had only recently been occupied by the Wari, began to reassert itself and possibly even to rival Wari power. Wari expansion ended abruptly, and the capital was abandoned by AD800.

DOMINATING THE ALTIPLANO
The Tiwanaku power base emanated from the Titicaca Basin of southern Peru–northern Bolivia, at 3,850m (12,600ft) above sea level. Like Huari, the city was founded in the Early Intermediate Period and became the capital of a unified state established through conquest and economic domination. In its heyday it occupied 4.5 sq km (1,100 acres).

The earliest major constructions at the site were begun by AD200, and by AD500 Tiwanaku was the capital of a considerable empire within and beyond the Titicaca Basin, stretching east and west to the Bolivian lowlands, west and northwest to the Peruvian coast, and south into northern Chile. Its cultural and religious influence extended even farther. Its chief rival to the north was the Wari Empire, and the two empires 'met' at the La Raya pass south of Cuzco, which became a sort of buffer zone between them. Curiously, the prosperity of Tiwanaku endured for roughly a millennium, fortuitously matching the 1,000-year periods of ages in Andean cosmology.

Tiwanaku's core comprised ceremonial-religious-civic structures, including monumental buildings, gateways and stone sculptures exhibiting religious motifs and gods whose depiction shows obvious affinities to Chavín images.

This core, aligned east–west, was confined within a moat and was surrounded by residential compounds built of adobe bricks.

Tiwanku belief was a culmination of the religious antecedents that appear to have united the peoples of the Titicaca Basin from as early as 1000BC. Ceremonial architecture at Chiripa and Pukará, for example, heralds that at Tiwanku.

The location of the city appears to have been chosen deliberately both for its position in the midst of fertile land and for the perceived sacredness of the landscape. The surrounding natural features constituted every element regarded as sacred within Andean Area religion: the sacred waters of Lake Titicaca to the west, the snow-capped peaks of the sacred mountains to the east, and in the middle of the lake the sacred Island of the Sun and Island of the Moon.

A SHARED RELIGION

Much of the religious and mythological imagery of Wari and Tiwanaku was virtually identical and originated in much earlier times. Derivation from Chavín demonstrates the continuity of pan-Andean religious belief. Despite the two capitals' obvious military opposition, scholars have entertained the possibility that religious missionaries from one city visited the other. It might have been that the priests were willing to set politics aside and let religious beliefs transcend such matters.

Shared religious imagery included in particular the Staff Deity image, winged beings in profile (sometimes with falcon and condor heads) and severed trophy heads. Winged beings appear both accompanying the Staff Deity and independently, and seem to be running, floating, flying or kneeling. The frontal Staff Deity, with mask-like face, radiating head rays (sometimes ending in serpent heads), and dressed in tunic, belt and kilt,

Left: The so-called 'monk' monolith at Tiwanaku. Such large stone statues were believed by the Incas to represent a former race of giants from an earlier age.

Above: The ruins of Pikillaqta, the largest and southernmost Middle Horizon Wari highland city, which guarded the border between the Wari and Tiwanaku empires.

appears on pottery and architecture and might have been the prototype for the creator god Viracocha.

Despite this apparent religious unity, the focus of the religious imagery at Huari differed from that at Tiwanaku. At Huari it was applied primarily to portable objects, particularly to ceramics; at Tiwanaku it was applied to monumental stone architecture, but rarely appeared on pottery. Thus, while Wari ceramics spread the word far and wide, Tiwanaku imagery was more confined to standing monuments in the capital and a few other sites. Similarly, religious ceremony at Huari appears to have been more private and confined to smaller groups, judging by its architecture, while at Tiwanaku it seems to have been more public and to have taken place inside large compounds designed for the purpose. Tiwanaku's bold pyramidal platforms and huge sunken courts contrast starkly with the repetitious, incremental, unit-like constructions at Huari.

KINGDOMS AND SHRINES

The Late Intermediate Period is defined by the break-up of the Wari and Tiwanaku empires. Once again political fragmentation prevailed in the Andean Area while, as in earlier periods, a certain pan-Andean religious unity persisted.

BREAK-UP AND RIVALRY

In the Altiplano, the Tiwanaku state succumbed to a multitude of smaller city-states collectively known as the Aymara Kingdoms: Colla, Lupaka, Cana, Canchi, Umasuyo and Pacaje. Rivalry was stirred up, and this was perpetuated by repeated droughts from about AD1100 through the next 400 years as El Niño weather events and consequent adverse environmental conditions affected Lake Titicaca's water level and the productivity of the surrounding land.

In the central and northern sierra the first glimmerings of what would become the Inca culture began to manifest themselves in distinctive art styles in the Cuzco Valley. People in these regions abandoned many of the cities and towns

Below: The great ramp to the summit of the temple to Pachacamc and one of its numerous surrounding courts.

in the valleys and moved to higher, moister locations, and towards the wetter eastern Cordillera. Competing centres protected the resources of their immediate areas: Pikillaqta (a southern Wari survival), Chokepukio (Wari's nearest inheritor), and clusters of settlements of ethnic groups known as Lucre, Killke, Wanka (whose capital was Wari Wanka) and Campa, and the Gran Pajaten city in Chachapoyas. Petty rivalry and temporary alliances were typical.

Along the central and southern Andean Area coasts the periods of drought affecting the highlands were even more severe. It was precarious enough in such desert coasts, but stress increased when irrigation systems failed as run-off from the mountains was further reduced. Mountain cities, by contrast, were able to survive on rainfall agriculture. The stress and decline of coastal centres incited local rivalry and the establishment of numerous small polities fighting for survival: Chiribaya, Ica and Chancay.

THE KINGDOM OF CHIMÚ

Two of the most prominent centres that stand out and perhaps typify this period were Chimú – or the Kingdom of Chimú

Above: For this Chimú wooden and mother-of-pearl jaguar figurine, a Pacific shell was used to create the coat of a rainforest animal living thousands of kilometres (miles) away.

– and Pachacamac. As in the Early Intermediate Period, these centres of power were coast-based.

The Chimú were the inheritors of Early Intermediate Period Moche power in the Moche and Lambayeque valleys. Duplicating the Moche pattern, the Chimú conquered to north and south, invading and subduing the northern Peruvian coastal valleys from the sea. Through later Inca records, historians of Chimú encounter legends of early kings of Chimú and the earlier dynasty founded by the legendary ruler Naymlap and ending with the disastrous reign of Fempellec.

The Kingdom of Chimú was the largest Andean Area state up to its time. At its height it controlled two-thirds of all irrigated land on the desert coasts, while elsewhere states were more localized.

Some scholars believe that the term 'Kingdoms' of Chimú is more appropriate, as the nature of the valley politics indicates that there may have been dual or multiple rulership among them. Inca records gleaned by the Spanish conquistadors describe two dynasties: Taycanamu at Chan Chan in the Moche Valley and Naymlap in the Lambayeque Valley. In the latter, it is tempting to equate the rich burials of the Sicán Lords with the descendants of Naymlap.

CHAN CHAN OF THE CHIMÚ

The fantastic site of Chan Chan, capital of the Taycanamu rulers, was founded around AD1000. It comprised a massive complex of individual compounds covering an area of 6 sq km (1,480 acres), around which domestic and workshop suburbs spread to cover 20 sq km (4,940 acres) in total. Each walled compound (known as a *ciudadela*) of the central core was rectangular in plan, its long axis oriented north–south, and made of thick walls up to 9m (29½ft) high of poured adobe mud. Most had only one entrance, on the north side, guarded by painted wooden human figures set in niches on either side. Each court contained the residences of the reigning Chimú king, his retainers and officials. Around other courtyards within the compounds were store rooms, U-shaped structures called *audiencias*, and burial platforms. Adjacent wings contained rooms for service and maintenance retainers, as well as walled-in wells.

From the historical records we know the names of at least three Chimú deities: the creator god Ai Apaec, the moon

Below: The Tschudi complex: even the walls of smaller enclosures within the ciudadelas *of the Chimú capital at Chan Chan were carefully moulded with geometric decoration.*

Above: The great temple-platform at Pachacamac – a huge pyramid of adobe bricks that grew to the size of a hill.

goddess Si and the sea god Ni. Chimú religious imagery merges Moche and Wari styles, and continues the long Chavín traditions of fanged beings, jaguars and serpentine images.

THE CULT OF PACHACAMAC

The site of Pachacamac on the central Peruvian coast was established in the Early Intermediate Period. In the wake of Chavín decline, it rose to prominence as a cult and pilgrimage site in the later half of the period, from about AD250. It was at this time that the first phases of the pyramid-platform to the sun and adjoining Temple to Pachacamac were built and presumably when the cult statues were installed. The name itself, in Quechua, means 'earth-maker'.

As a centre of local political power in the Middle Horizon, Pachacamac succumbed to Wari conquest, but as a religious cult centre it weathered the period of subjugation to persist as a cult and pilgrimage centre for more than 1,000 years through the Late Intermediate Period into Inca times. As a creator god, Pachacamac was the only serious rival to Viracocha, supreme god of the Inca, for that title.

CONQUEST AND EMPIRE: THE INCAS

The final chronological period of ancient Andean Area history is the Late Horizon, which began about AD1400. It is marked by the rise of the Inca and their domination of the Andean Area, forming the largest empire ever known in the New World. Inca hegemony lasted a mere 132 years, however, until it met its match in cunning and military guile in the person of Francisco Pizarro.

EARLY BEGINNINGS

Inca beginnings were in the early Late Intermediate Period. During the political fragmentation of that period, the Inca were one of several local tribes or ethnic groups competing for survival within the Cuzco region and among numerous city-states scattered throughout the sierra. From the founding of the Inca ruling dynasty by the legendary Manco Capac in the mid-13th century, the Inca began to conquer the sierra and coastal regions and to unify them into a state in which central control was paramount. As with earlier Andean states, military conquest

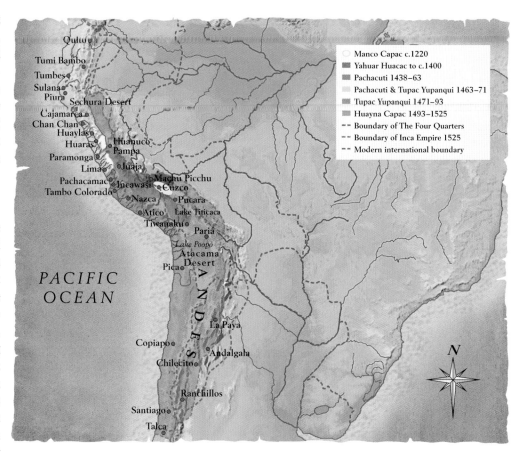

Above: Map showing extent of the Inca Empire and the Four Quarters from the time of the legendary founder Manco Capac to the rule of Huayna Capac in the 16th century.

Legend:
- Manco Capac c.1220
- Yahuar Huacac to c.1400
- Pachacuti 1438–63
- Pachacuti & Tupac Yupanqui 1463–71
- Tupac Yupanqui 1471–93
- Huayna Capac 1493–1525
- Boundary of The Four Quarters
- Boundary of Inca Empire 1525
- Modern international boundary

Below: A carved wooden face on a post from the Inca coastal regions, c.1400.

brought economic regulation and compulsory state religion. Both impositions on the losing parties were made more palatable through long-surviving traditional pan-Andean religious concepts, and by the incorporation of local deities, cults and religious practices into existing versions and the inclusion of local rulers in Inca government.

Manco Capac and his successors first defeated local rivals within the Cuzco Valley. The threat of their arch-enemy, the Chancas, nearly ended this early progress when they marched on Cuzco in 1438. The crushing of the Chancas by Pachacuti Inca Yupanqui, steeped in legend and the source of some of the most sacred *huaca* sites around the city, secured Inca domination of their immediate territory.

It was from this date that the Incas began their rapid expansion throughout the Andean Area. The date highlights the fact that the empire endured less than 100 years as the pre-eminent power in Andean America.

DOUBLING THE EMPIRE

Pachacuti ruled until 1471. His first campaigns subdued the city-states of the central Andes north to Huánuco and south to the northern and western shores of Lake Titicaca. The biggest prize of all was the conquest of the Kingdom of Chimú, which occurred in 1470–1. Together with his son and principal heir, Tupac Yupanqui (The Unforgettable One), Pachacuti doubled the size of the Inca Empire in less than ten years, incorporating Chimú and beyond into what is now Ecuador.

Above: Inca warriors attacking a fortress during their many campaigns of conquest, shown in Nueva Crónica y Buen Gobierno.

Upon his succession, Tupac Yupanqui more than doubled the size of the empire again, in 22 years of long and ruthless campaigns – to the coast west of Cuzco and to the farthest southern reaches, into modern Chile and Argentina. Upon his death, the throne was briefly disputed. Once secured by Huayna Capac, one of Tupac's sons, his reign (1493–1525) was occupied principally with campaigns to fill in corners in the northern provinces, mainly in the eastern Andean foothills and selva, with consolidation of Pachacuti's and Tupac's conquests, and with putting down local rebellions. Huayna Capac's attempts to conquer the selva had limited success.

KEYS TO SUCCESS

The success of Inca rapid expansion and domination lies in what had been established and entrenched in Andean political, social and economic structures before then. The Middle Horizon Wari and Tiwanaku empires, the former including the Cuzco region, had consolidated (as did the Late Intermediate Period Chimú) principles of centralized political control, organized through a network of administrative centres, roads and rapid communication. The practice of labour tax used levies of workers to co-ordinate labour distribution; it was an annual obligation to the central government. Such structures enabled the gathering, storage and redistribution of goods and the exchange of commodities between highland and lowland regions, ensuring the prosperity of all.

The Incas reconstituted these systems where their remnants remained and imported them into regions where they had not formerly existed. They maintained political power through the control of resources and the practice of resettling large groups of people around the provinces, and by using existing local chiefs to administer their command and removing to Cuzco the sons of local rulers, to hold hostage.

The nature of pan-Andean religious belief reinforced the Inca's 'right to rule' through the incorporation of local deities and icons into the state religion. At the same time it imposed the official state cult of Inti – the sun – personified by the Sapa Inca himself. In addition to hostages, the Incas took regional sacred objects to the capital; and craftsmen from the provinces were removed to Cuzco to construct buildings and produce imperial goods for the royal household.

Right: On this Moche pot, two warriors probably engage in ritual combat while one of them holds a decapitated head.

ELEMENTS OF COLLAPSE

Perhaps inevitably, strains and tensions within such a vast and diverse empire brought successional rivalry. It had happened when Tupac died, and when Huayna Capac died, a bitter civil war broke out between his two sons Huáscar and Atahualpa. This was the situation in which Francisco Pizarro arrived on his third visit, in 1532.

Manipulating this disruption, Pizarro was able to bring the empire to its knees with a few hundred Spaniards. He exploited resentment in the recently conquered provinces to gain native allies, he played one royal faction against the other in the dispute over succession and used the assassination of one brother, Huáscar, by the other, Atahualpa, to imprison the latter and demand a huge ransom that bankrupted the empire. By such methods the Spaniards kept the Incas off balance. As the empire's cohesion crumbled, the alliances, social organization and economic structure of the empire were reconfigured to suit Spanish greed and rule. Feeble revolts attempting to reinstate Inca power were quickly crushed by increasing Spanish might in the new colony.

THEMES AND PEOPLES

The earliest sites of human habitation in the Andean Area date to about 11,500 years ago. It has been biologically demonstrated that the inhabitants of the New World descend from three or four distinct populations and several incidents of migration into North America, but that migrants into the South American continent all descend from only one of these groups.

The diverse landscape and regional variety of the Andean Area encouraged technological, social and economic innovation. As the hunter-gatherer lifestyle of the earliest Lithic Period evolved into an era of farming and permanent settlement, people adapted differently to the challenges provided by the coastal and mountain environments, and many different cultures developed throughout the Andes from the late Initial Period onwards.

Different languages also developed, and linguists have identified major language groups within this area. Indeed, throughout South America they estimate as many as 2,000 languages were once spoken, though only about 600 have been attested.

Recognition of the existence of different peoples among ancient Andeans is revealed in their many stories of the origins of humankind. In one story, the creator god Viracocha shaped men and women from clay then painted them in different colours, wearing different styles of clothing, and gave them their languages, cultural practices, songs, arts and crafts, and the knowledge of agriculture to distinguish between the different tribes and nations.

Left: The eastern façade and entrance to the Temple of the Cult of Chavín, the first great ancient Andean pilgrimage centre.

CIVIC-CEREMONIAL CENTRES

Two principal themes characterized pre-Hispanic Andean civilization: a general unity through shared religious beliefs across the Andean Area, and a settlement pattern of independent yet linked communities. From the earliest farming villages, through the construction of monumental civic-ceremonial centres of increasing complexity, to the establishment and growth of cities, universal patterns developed in cross-regional trade, shared methods of craftsmanship and organized political and social systems of labour. This was for growing crops and for the production of pottery, textiles, metalwork and other artefacts. With detailed variation, these universal patterns gave developmental impetus to the process and progress of Andean civilization.

ARCHITECTURAL 'TRADITIONS'

Different 'traditions' of civic-ceremonial architecture developed in tropical, desert coastal and sierra settings. Within varied lifestyles, regional cultures centralized religious belief and integrated labour to build special places for communal worship. These special places held sacred objects that represented the gods, and some places became sites of pilgrimage serving large regions. Eventually, a select few became the most important pilgrimage centres, some of them enduring for long periods.

In the forested north (now in Ecuador), Valdivia Tradition settlements were characterized by central oval or circular plazas, with domed oval communal structures surrounded by houses. Sometimes the communal buildings were on top of low earthen mounds. One type, known as a 'charnel house', was for mortuary ritual, to prepare corpses for burial elsewhere; a second type, called a 'fiesta house', was for feasting and drinking.

In the coastal valleys of northern and central Peru the establishment of civic-ceremonial centres became a mainstay of Andean civilization from about 2850BC. Known as the Supe-Aspero Tradition and the El Paraíso Tradition, they take their names from the 17-mound centres in the Río Supe Valley and the site of Aspero, and from El Paraíso. Both traditions featured raised mounds that provided flat, open spaces on top for congregational ritual and to support complex multi-chambered structures. Ceremony seems to have emphasized public-oriented activity, the flat top providing a stage for the ritual to be viewed by a large congregation assembled in front of the mound. Within this cohesive theme there was considerable variation in the sizes and shapes of coastal platforms and in the building complexes on top. Ceremony involved burnt offerings, but the locations and contexts of these varied.

REGIONAL CENTRES

The extensive platforms at Salinas de Chao, Los Morteros and Piedra Parada lack surrounding domestic remains, indicating that they were built as venues for communal ritual by the peoples of surrounding settlements. The extensive 17-mound complex of the Supe Valley also suggests regional worship, and perhaps influence beyond. If true, the extended 'site' was the earliest in a long Andean tradition of pilgrimage sites. In contrast, at Río Seco, Bandurria, Culebras, Huaynuna and Huaca Prieta the modest sizes of the ceremonial structures

Left: Desert coastal oases valleys, where water was precious, developed ritual centres alongside sophisticated irrigation systems.

Right: Reconstruction of the circular sunken court and the terraced platforms built against the hill slope at Salinas de Chao.

and associated domestic buildings and refuse indicates that they were built by and largely for their local communities.

Many chambers in the complexes on top of Supe-Aspero platforms included rectangular niches, possibly for sacred objects. At Caral, the ceremonial complex includes an element of exclusion where it enclosed a large walled plaza with a 'fire altar' in one corner; another chamber housed a sacred obelisk. At Huaynuna, Piedra Parada and Caral there is evidence of contact with sierra ritual in the construction of oval ceremonial chambers and sunken courtyards. Room complexes of later building phases at some sites feature bilateral symmetry.

ASPERO

The largest of the Supe sites, Aspero, comprises an extensive mound complex: six major flat platforms and 11 lower (1–2m/3–6½ft) mounds surrounded by 15ha (37 acres) of public and domestic remains. The larger mounds rise up to 4m (12ft) above the valley floor, or 10m (32ft) where banked against the side or top of a hill. Two of these, Huaca de los Idolos and Huaca de los Sacrificios, produced radio-carbon dates as early as 3055 and 2850BC respectively. Both platforms underwent several phases of covering and later enlargement.

Right: A figurine of unbaked clay, which was deliberately broken and buried at Huaca de los Idolos. The fragmentary figure is shown in the first two drawings; the drawing on the right shows a projected reconstruction.

The free-standing platform at Huaca de los Sacrificios included an elite, textile-wrapped ritual infant burial, apparently accompanied by an adult sacrifice, showing that social hierarchy had clearly become established. At Huaca de los Idolos, one ritual chamber on top of the platform included a buried cache of 13 or more deliberately broken clay figurines.

EL PARAISO

The largest Preceramic Period stone-built civic-ceremonial centre was El Paraíso. Radiocarbon dates of 2000BC and later indicate that its civic-ceremonial complex represents a transitional stage from the Preceramic traditions and the Initial Period U-shaped complexes described earlier. It comprised two long parallel raised platforms (250 x 50m/820 x 140ft) forming the sides of a U framing a 7ha (17 acre) plaza. The base of the U comprises several smaller ruins rather than a central platform. Other masonry complexes were built near by as El Paraíso expanded. Evidence of fire ritual and an absence of domestic debris around the ceremonial complexes indicate that El Paraíso was built as a ritual centre for people living throughout a larger region.

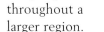

COMMUNAL RITUAL: KOTOSH

Farming community peoples in the mountain valleys of central and northern Peru also cultivated communal ritual by building large communal structures. While the environment of isolated valleys was conducive to social division and variation between valleys, the development of similar corporate constructions demonstrates social union and amalgamation, reveals contact among valleys and reveals underlying common religious belief here as well. To build such structures required political control and the mobilization of communal labour. The buildings must also have served civic and administrative purposes.

THE KOTOSH TRADITION

Ritual and special-purpose architecture in the sierra is known as the Kotosh Tradition, after the type-site, Kotosh, situated at about 2,000m (6,600ft) above sea level, in a region of temperate climate and limited seasonal rainfall in the eastern Andes. Its location typifies lower sierra village settlement and offered access to the natural resources of both higher and lower ecological zones. The early Kotosh economy was mainly hunting and gathering – there are many chipped stone tools and debris, and charred seeds, but at first no evidence of cultivated plants. Anatomical changes on the animal bones found at Kotosh show that guinea pigs and llamas were domesticated, or at least kept and herded. Deer bones show that hunting remained an important source of meat.

Like coastal architectural traditions, Kotosh sites featured platform mounds. These mounds, however, were more standardized in shape and size, and served as platforms for structures of a more excluding nature. A characteristic of the Kotosh tradition was the raising of a large twin ceremonial mound complex, indicating the early establishment of social division into two kin-related groups.

Excavations at Kotosh reveal long periods of use, perhaps

Above: As a staple of life, maize and other crops exemplified Pacha Mama (Mother Earth), from which all life sprang.

through generations, comprising ten superimposed constructions. Early mounds were built by people who made no pottery, and the later mounds were made by their pottery-making Initial Period and Early Horizon descendants.

A second Kotosh form was the sunken court or plaza (*plazas hundidas*). Every platform mound and plaza was a place of protocol and designed behaviour. People participated in the construction of these non-subsistence buildings and in prescribed ritual activity, presumably led by religious specialists.

The contemporary site of La Galgada, in the central sierra north of Kotosh, demonstrates similar characteristics. At about 1,100m (3,600ft) above sea level and located roughly equidistantly between the Pacific coast and the semi-tropical eastern selva, it too exploited both zones for ornamental products. La Galgada burials

Above:
Reconstruction of
the aerial view of the
mound-top chambers at La Galgada.
It is not known if such temples were roofed.

contain shell beads and discs from the coast and Amazonian tropical bird feathers from the east. The La Galgada economy was demonstrably based on farming. There are remains of domesticated beans, squashes, fruits, chilli peppers, gourds, cotton and a single maize cob. Remains of ancient irrigation canals are consistent with the necessity of irrigation to grow these plants.

POSITIVE AND NEGATIVE SPACES

Platforms and sunken courts organize space in two distinct ways. Platforms are positive structures – exterior and elevated. They divide space vertically and support hierarchical buildings for special purposes. The mounds themselves, and more especially their buildings, hide ritual from the general populace and render them exclusive to specialists. Sunken courts, on the other hand, constitute negative space – interior and secluded. Their walls restrict space and confine activities within them. At most sites both platforms and sunken courts were built, though at a few sites only a sunken court was built.

SOCIAL DIVISIONS

The ceremonial constructions at La Galgada, as at Kotosh, comprise twin mounds surrounded by dwellings, again indicating a two-part social division. Each mound has a main central platform and subsidiary buildings. Each comprises a series of superimposed mounds and buildings, and the larger platform produced radiocarbon dates ranging between 2200 and 1200BC.

Both Kotosh and La Galgada were clearly sites of regional importance. The presence of exotic commodities at both sites implies the beginnings of exchange between coast and sierra and between sierra and tropics – a tradition so characteristic of later Andean civilization. Their inhabitants had succeeded in achieving an economy and lifestyle that afforded them the time to

marshal their labour for the purely non-subsistence activity of special architecture, religiously focused sites and special burials. These constructions, to their builders' minds, were vital to the continuity of their existence and were the earliest such sites in an Andean tradition of meeting such existential or religious needs in this way.

THE CHINCHORROS

Much farther south of the coastal and sierra traditions, sites on the desert coast of Peru and northern Chile reveal a singular economy based on the riches of the sea. Chemical analysis of the bones of the inhabitants of the culture shows a diet of 90 per cent marine foods. So rich were

Above: The ritual honouring of important ancestors began perhaps with mummification among the Chinchorros of northern Chile.

the marine resources that large towns could be supported with little or no farming of edible cultigens. Coastal floodplain plants were gathered and later cultivated for fuel, clothing fibre, shelter, water craft, nets, fishing line and floats, basketry and other tools for marine exploitation.

Chinchorros domestic structures include burials of the earliest mummified bodies, preserved with salt and reed-mat wrappings, presaging the Andean traditions of both mummification and burial among the living to keep the deceased as part of the present.

EXCHANGE OF GOODS AND IDEAS

The architectural traditions of Kotosh, Supe-Aspero and El Paraíso reveal the beginnings of an exchange that became characteristically Andean. It involved the interchange of both commodities and religious ideas within and between geographical zones: among respective regions at similar heights (horizontal exchange) and between highland and lowland communities, such as sierra and coast and sierra and selva (vertical exchange).

DISTRIBUTION AND EXCHANGE

The exchange of goods became a necessity in Andean civilization for the trading and obtaining of either key products that could not be grown in one zone or another or exotic materials that were native to one zone or another.

Adaptation within Andean civilization was shaped by the distribution of natural resources and by the limits within which various domesticated plants and animals could be grown, reared and herded. For example, food staples such as maize can be grown at altitudes up to about 3,000m

(9,800ft), but are at risk from frost and hail; crops frequently fail. Maize domestication and cultivation thus spread from coast to highlands. In contrast, the potato, originally a highland crop, was eventually cultivated throughout a range from nearly sea level to 3,800m (12,500ft). A similar division into zones applies to growing cotton and herding llamas and alpacas for meat and wool. Tropical fruits and lowland products such as peanuts, avocados, manioc, chillies and squashes were redistributed among zones through trade as they became part of Andean Area culture.

In coastal desert oases, resources were similar despite the

Left: Exotic objects, such as this Pacific spiny or thorny oyster, were traded from the far northern coasts to the highlands.

Above: Highland staples, particularly the potato, also became lowland staples through trade between the two areas.

long coastline. The same is true of vast tropical lowlands. Environmental similarities are reinforced by limited annual temperature fluctuation. These factors contribute to exchange within and between valleys or selva regions. At increasing elevation, however, seasonal variation increases and growing periods shorten. In highland areas, zones of cultivation are compressed and stacked within the environment. Highland peoples consequently practise greater vertical movement within these zones to pursue cultivation in basins and valleys and herding in the Altiplano. These factors contribute to exchange between communities at different altitudes within the highlands and also between highlands and lowlands.

AVAILABILITY AND DEMAND

It is frequently the case in the Andean Area that where abundant flatlands (potentially useful for crop-growing) occur, there is less rainfall, a threat of drought and a need to irrigate. In contrast,

Above: The decorations on many Moche pots depict scenes of daily life. Here a fisherman sets out in a balsa boat.

highland zones have greater rainfall and are less affected by drought, but flat lands suitable for agriculture are more restricted and there is a need to increase growing space by terracing. For these different reasons both zones required the input of organized labour as populations increased. However, fewer than 20 per cent of major Andean cultivated plants grow above 3,000m (9,800ft), while 90 per cent thrive best below 1,000m (3,300ft). This inversion of available land and crop diversity created a perennial strain on supply and demand, and it is this tension that underlays exchange between peoples at different elevations in ancient Andean civilization.

MOVEMENT OF PEOPLE

Exchange was not only of goods but also of peoples, adapting to different land zones to exploit cultivation possibilities. Andean highland peoples regularly exploited irrigated farmlands for maize, cotton, peppers, gourds and squashes in a lowland zone, in middle-zone potato lands and in Altiplano herding pastures. Furthermore, evidence in Inca times shows that the peoples in these zones were kin-related groups with a regularized system of obligations and duties to the whole group.

Among coastal valley and plain cultures the sea provided a natural highway for the movement of goods and peoples up and down the coast. The Moche kingdom, for example, was a seafaring nation that pursued conquest from one valley to another by sea invasion.

As regions came under the control of larger political entities, the redistribution of products required greater regulation and intricate administration. To maintain economic balance, both products and labour needed control and regulation. Later imperial cultures, and ultimately the Incas, practised active transportation of peoples within the empire and colonization of regions to obtain materials from distant areas or exotic locations.

RITUAL GOODS AND IDEAS

To maintain religious integrity and appease the gods, and so secure the well-being of humans, rulers needed to obtain exotic raw materials considered essential for ritual. Thus, tropical products such as tobacco, coca and forest mushrooms required not only secured sources but also organization and security in transport. The use of cotton and llama wool textiles at coastal and highland sites, and of coastal shells (including *Spondylus princeps* – the spiny or thorny oyster from Ecuador and farther north) in highland ceremonial contexts confirms the early beginnings of both horizontal and vertical exchange. As weaving became an entrenched part of Andean cultural expression and part of state control, the redistribution of cotton and wool became heavily regulated in Inca times and was no doubt equally regulated in earlier kingdoms.

The exchange of exotic products across such distant regions implies the exchange of ideas associated with the items and their suppliers. The nature of both highland and coastal ceremonial architecture from the earliest Preceramic times shows recognition of mountain, earth and sea gods throughout Andean cultures, and the association of them in ritual structures.

Below: From ancient times, coastal valley oases probably consisted of numerous small growing fields sharing an irrigation system.

CONFLICT AND CO-OPERATION

Coastal El Paraíso was the first example of the U-shaped ceremonial complex that became the hallmark of Initial Period civic-ceremonial architecture. This period showed both the start of a widespread similarity in civic-ceremonial construction and signs of conflict between political units. These are manifestations of the two alternating themes of political cohesion and fragmentation in Andean civilization.

The combination of platform mounds and sunken courts in the late Preceramic Period at Kotosh, La Galgada and coastal sites may have constituted a Kotosh Religious Tradition, perhaps the first widespread Andean 'religion'. Scholars speculate that to agricultural people the sunken court was the focus for veneration of the Pacha Mama (Mother Earth), or even for the ritual re-enactment of creation or birth in a descent into the court and re-emergence from it. Where both structures were built, the sunken court was situated before the ascending staircase of the platform, its own staircase aligned to it. This combination – the elevated and

Above: When peoples gather to trade their produce, ideas are also exchanged and bonds developed between different regions.

the subterranean – suggests rituals that proceeded from a descent into Mother Earth followed by an ascent into the sky to the father Apu (or vice versa perhaps).

FARMING AND RITUAL

In the early centuries of the third millennium BC, climatic improvement and increased rainfall fostered the spread of intensive agriculture throughout the Andean Area. Intensive agriculture with irrigation works at coastal sites was added to maritime exploitation.

Agriculture and pastoralism spread into the higher sierra and Altiplano, including the Titicaca Basin. Increasing population and agricultural production, and the exploitation of new lands, brought economic prosperity. Easier living created time for increased sophistication of political structure and for concern with religious concepts.

Left: Conflict between city-states is evident from at least the Initial Period in stone sculptures of warriors, as at Cerro Sechín.

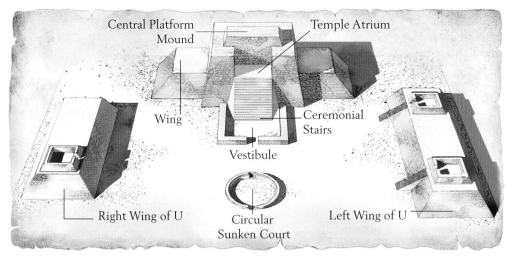

Central Platform
Mound

Temple Atrium

Wing

Ceremonial
Stairs

Vestibule

Right Wing of U

Circular
Sunken Court

Left Wing of U

Above: A U-shaped temple showing the large central platform mound flanked by left and right wings and a circular sunken court.

Intensive agriculture, manifested by irrigation works and concern for rain and run-off water, may have fostered increased veneration of Mother Earth, Pacha Mama, and of mountain deities represented by Apu. Increased concern with the Milky Way (Mayu) accompanied the need to track the movements of stars and planets for agricultural scheduling.

These concerns brought an unprecedented spate of civic-ceremonial complex-building throughout the Andean Area. As in the Preceramic Period, Initial Period coastal complexes were small and local and also vast, presumably to serve a wide region. There were scores of complexes throughout the valleys. New phases of building at Kotosh, La Galgada and El Paraíso created U-shaped complexes at the last two sites about 1900 and 2000BC respectively. Sunken courts changed from circular to rectangular.

The largest Initial Period civic-ceremonial complex was at Sechín Alto in the coastal Casma Valley. Begun around 1400BC, the huge platform forming the base of its U-shaped complex was 300m (980ft) long and 250m (820ft) wide and still stands 40m (130ft) above the plain. Platforms forming the arms of the U flank a succession of plazas, including two circular sunken courts, in an area 400m (1,300ft) wide by 1,100m (3,600ft) long.

Right: Co-operation within and between cities enabled people to build and maintain extensive field terraces and irrigation systems.

Surrounding this complex was 10.5 sq km (2,600 acres) of buildings and smaller platforms. Other classic coastal U-shaped centres included Huaca de los Reyes, Cardal, La Florida, San Jacinto and Garagay.

SIGNS OF CONFLICT

Accompanying this unity in architectural form were signs of conflict between the political units associated with different civic-ceremonial centres, or perhaps between valleys. Cladding their ceremonial mounds with hand-made mud bricks, the builders of different sites vied with each other to decorate them with enormous adobe friezes, often painting them in rich colours. Two smaller, yet imposing, sites exemplify theses developments, both in the Sechín–Casma Valley.

Cerro Sechín was a multi-roomed sanctuary adorned with adobe friezes painted with felines and fish. About 1200BC, this complex was filled to make a large rectangular platform surrounded by a facing of incised megaliths. Two processions of armed warriors carry axe-like clubs and march from the sides around the front of the building to converge on the main entrance. On either side of the entrance, monoliths depict fluttering banners.

A few kilometres (miles) away, Llamas-Moxeke is dominated by two huge rectangular platforms about 1km (½ mile) apart and equidistant from a square court. The Moxeke platform, 25m (82ft) high and 165m (540ft) on each side, had a façade decorated with huge niches framing high-relief friezes painted red, blue, white and black. Figures depicted include two human faces, two richly dressed individuals and a person with his back turned out and arms bound behind him as if a prisoner.

The coastal flowering lasted until about 900BC, from which time a period of drought took severe effect and almost all coastal ceremonial complexes were abandoned within a century or two. Sierra ceremonial complexes faired better, many remaining functional into the last few centuries BC, into the Early Horizon. The rise of a new highland U-shaped ceremonial centre, Chavín de Huántar, hailed the beginning of an ecumenical Andean religion that was widespread and enduring.

RELIGIOUS COHESION

The common use of platforms, U-shaped complexes and the association of sunken courts suggests religious ecumenicalism, and use both for ritual and civic functions – even that the two activities were functionally intertwined. A Kotosh Religious Tradition has earlier been suggested.

In the succeeding Early Horizon, while coastal centres remained modest after centuries of drought began to abate, one sierra centre arose that without question became a cult and pilgrimage centre. It was the 'cathedral' of Andean religion and included all the classic features that had been developed in earlier periods in coastal and sierra traditions. This was Chavín de Huántar.

THE RISE OF CHAVÍN DE HUÁNTAR

From about 900BC, as coastal ceremonial centres were abandoned, Chavín de Huántar rose to prominence. It was not urban in size or layout and lacked a surrounding domestic district. Instead it comprised a modest complex to accommodate a small population of priests, officials, artisans, servants and pilgrims to support and serve its cult. Its influence stretched throughout the central and northern Andes, and west and east to the coast and tropical lowlands. Further, it played a crucial role in the dissemination of technology. Its central location appears to have established and perpetuated its importance.

At its largest, the Chavín de Huántar ceremonial centre covered about 42ha (104 acres), with 2,000–3,000 inhabitants. The Old Temple framed a circular sunken courtyard. Scores of sculpted heads project from its four-storey stone walls. The temple interior comprises a labyrinth of interconnecting narrow passages and chambers, the southern wing of which was later doubled in size as the site flourished, and is known as the New Temple, although both temples were used simultaneously after the expansion.

MONOLITHIC SCULPTURE

In one interior gallery stands the stone idol called the Lanzón (after its lance-like shape) or Great Image, probably the earliest pan-Andean oracle: a carved granite monolith 4.5m (15ft) high. The Lanzón faces east and portrays a humanoid form, but overall depicts a monster visage. Its right hand is raised and its left lowered by its side; its feet and hands end in claws. Its mouth is thick-lipped, drawn in a hideous snarl and punctuated by long, outward-curving canines. Its eyebrows and hair end in serpent heads; its earlobes hang heavy with pendants. It wears a tunic and headdress, both of which are decorated with feline heads. Its notched top protrudes through the ceiling into an upper gallery in which priests probably sat in secrecy, projecting their voices as that of the god.

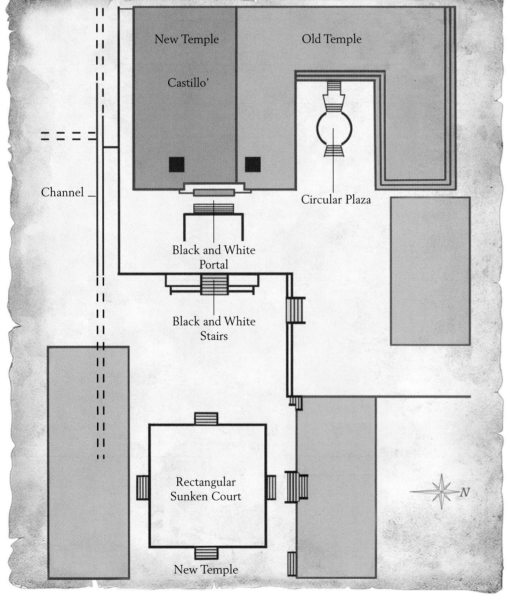

Left: Plan of Chavín de Huántar, one of the most elaborate ceremonial centres of its period, with its U-shaped temples.

CULT CENTRE

That Chavín de Huántar was the site of a cult seems indisputable. In a gallery next to the sunken plaza, excavators found 800 broken ceramic vessels decorated in styles from cultures as far apart as the northern coast to the central highlands. Scattered among bowls and containers were llama, deer, guinea pig and fish bones – thought to have been either offerings or a store of ritual trappings for ceremonies.

Chavín iconography drew its inspiration from both the natural world – animals, plants and aquatic life – and a variety of ecological zones – the ocean, coast, the mountains and tropical lowlands. The Tello Obelisk is a low-relief carved granite monolith 2.5m (8ft) high, in the shape of a supernatural cayman. Notched at the top like the Lanzón, it probably also stood upright in a gallery or courtyard. Additional carvings on and around the cayman depict plants and animals, including peanuts and manioc from the tropical lowlands and *Strombus* and *Spondylus* shells of species native to the Ecuadorian coast, attesting to the wide influence of the Chavín Cult. Other carvings depict jaguars, serpents, and harpy or crested eagles.

As the cult's fame spread and the site was enlarged, ceramic styles and other exotic foods, plants and animals continued to inspire its artistic imagery. Evidence from the domestic buildings shows the development of social hierarchy in the unequal distribution of goods and of craft specialization. The cult supported artisans applying its symbolism to portable artefacts and spreading it through exchange, thereby expanding and entrenching the cult.

With the expansion of the south wing of the temple, the imagery became more elaborate. The relief of a new supreme deity was erected in the patio of the New Temple. Like the Lanzón, this is a humanoid figure with a fanged mouth, multiple bracelets, anklets and ear pendants. It holds a *Strombus* shell in its right hand and a *Spondylus* shell in its left hand.

THE STAFF DEITY

Another huge carved stone slab, the Raimondi Stela (2m/6½ft long), depicts a deity who in some ways epitomizes the cult: the Staff God/Goddess. Ubiquitous

Left: The Raimondi Stela at Chavín de Huántar is the ultimate representation of the Staff Deity. It can be read either way up.

Above: The ray-encircled Staff Deity is the central figure on the Gateway of the Sun in the Kalasasaya enclosure at Tiwanaku.

in Chavín iconography, this figure was portrayed with male or female attributes. The full-frontal, standing figure is a composite of animal and human characteristics. Like those of other Chavín deities, the hands and feet of this figure end in claws, the mouth displays huge curved fangs and the ears are bedecked with ornaments. The arms are outstretched and clutch staffs in one form or another, themselves elaborately festooned with spikes and plume-like decorations.

The exact significance and meaning of the Staff Deity is unknown. That he/she was a powerful deity is attested by the application of the image all over Chavín de Huántar on stones and walls, and throughout the central Andes and coast on portable objects, including ceramics and textiles. The potency of the Staff Deity is likewise demonstrated by the fact that the imagery of a frontal, staff-bearing deity endured from the Early Horizon until Inca times. Given this exceptional importance, it seems certain that the Staff Deity was a supernatural being with a distinct 'personality', possibly a primeval creator god.

PEOPLES OF THE EMPIRE

Spanish administrative and judicial archives contain chronicles and records of the Inca conquest of numerous ethnic groups, chiefdoms and political units called *señorios*. From these sources we have a veritable roster of the peoples of the empire.

RIVALS OF THE INCAS

Guaman Poma de Ayala's history refers to the chiefdom of the Ayarmacas, one of the many politico-ethnic divisions of the Acamama region around Cuzco. As the first powerful Inca rivals, the Ayarmacas played an instrumental role in the founding of Cuzco. Poma de Ayala identifies 'some first Incas' called Tocay Capac and Pinahua Capac, whom other sources call 'kings', or identify as generic

Below: One of the greatest Inca conquests involved capturing the Chimú fortresses, such as that of coastal Paramonga.

titles for the rulers of two allied chiefdoms – Ayarmaca and Pinahua – comprising 18 towns south of Cuzco.

Prolonged Ayarmaca campaigns against the Incas of Cuzco resulted in stalemate. However, as the Incas subdued other neighbours and expanded within the valley, the Ayarmaca lords were relegated to the status of local chiefs within the Inca hierarchy. As the Incas wrestled for control, their new arch-rivals became the Chancas, whose defeat in 1438 was a defining point in the rise of the Inca state, and the traditional date for the beginning of the empire, along with Pachacuti Inca Yupanqui's ascent to the throne.

PEOPLES OF THE INCA EMPIRE

Pachacuti turned his attention to the Altiplano chiefdoms. His predecessor Viracocha had formed an alliance with the Lupaqas of Chucuito against the Hatun Colla, but

Above: Huayna Capac, 12th of the Inca dynasty and the last great conquering emperor, ruled from 1493 until 1526.

success against the Chancas changed Pachacuti's perspective on domination. The Collas were utterly defeated in battle, and the peace scene frequently depicted on *kero* drinking vessels shows the Collas wearing especially tall headdresses, emphasizing the cultural variety and distinction between ethnic groups. At the victory celebration in Cuzco, Pachacuti ordered the beheading of the Colla leaders, warning others who might resist.

The effect was immediate and the remaining Altiplano lords accepted Inca overlordship without further resistance. This Cuntisuyu quarter formed the core of the empire, incorporating the chiefdoms of the Soras, Lucanas, Andahuaylas, Canas, Canchis, Paucarcollas, Pacajes and Azángaros, and exposing the western coastal *señorio* of Collao.

The Chinchas of Collao submitted peacefully at the intimidating approach of Inca armies led by Tupac Yupanqui. Pachacuti and Tupac next expanded north, creating Chinchaysuyu quarter, valley chiefdoms falling one after another: the

Below: In less than 100 years, the Incas subdued peoples from Ecuador to Chile and from the Pacific to the Amazon Rainforest.

Guarco and Lunahuaná chiefdoms in the central Andes; the Collec *señorio*, including the Chuquitanta, Carabayllo, Zapan, Macas, Guaraui, Guancayo and Quivi chiefdoms; and the Ychsma *señorio*.

THE KINGDOM OF THE CHIMÚ

The Inca armies marched on the vast, ancient northern Kingdom of Chimú. Garcilasco de la Vega's *Comentarios Reales de los Incas* describes the confrontation:

The brave Chimú [Minchançaman], his arrogance and pride now tamed, appeared before the prince [Tupac Inca Yupanqui] with as much submission and humility, and grovelled on the ground before him, worshipping him and repeating the same request [for pardon] as he had made through his ambassadors. The prince received him affectionately in order to relieve [his] grief … [and] bade two of the captains raise him from the ground. After hearing him, [Tupac] told him that all that was past was forgiven. … The Inca had not come to deprive him of his estates and authority, but to improve his idolatrous religion, his laws, and his customs.

Unlike the treatment of Colla leaders, Tupac set a new precedent, incorporating new states and recognizing their integrity under Inca overlordship. Perhaps the size and importance of Chimú prompted special treatment.

Farther north, the coastal chiefdoms of the Quito, Cañaris, Huancavilcas, Manta and Puná were conquered; then the Huarochirí, Yauyos, and the *señorio* of Guzmango. These northern chiefdoms fell so rapidly that there was hardly time

Above: The centre of the empire was Cuzco, here seen from the fortress-temple of Sacsahuaman overlooking the city.

for incorporation and consolidation; archaeology and the chronicles, however, attest to the rapid imposition of Inca rule, installation of local elites as provincial governors and collection of tax produce into large centres for redistribution.

OUTSIDERS AND REBELS

The Incas also recognized peoples beyond imperial borders, against whom their campaigns were less successful. The chronicles of Tupac Yupanqui's incursions into the selva of Antisuyu quarter mention the Opataris, Manosuyu, Mañaris, Yanaximes, Chunchos and Paititi.

Many chiefdoms accepted diminution of their authority reluctantly. Tupac's son Huayna Capac campaigned against the Chiriguanas of Collasuyu quarter, and, in the far north, the Chachapoyas of Chinchaysuyu, the Caranquis, Otavalos, Cayambis, Cochasquis and Pifos, all of whom had rebelled. The Huanca of Chinchaysuyu allied themselves to Pizarro in a final bid to throw off Inca domination.

The Incas strove for political unity by utilizing local rulers and incorporating them into the Inca hierarchy, giving local elites and subjects a sense of belonging. Nevertheless, local independence had lasted for generations, so there was considerable resentment of Inca impositions, particularly among more far-flung peoples. This potential instability, especially at the death of Huayna Capac in 1526, played into Spanish hands.

POWER AND WARFARE

By the end of the Initial Period, civilization in the Andean Area had established an underlying unity in religious concepts and some basic civic-ceremonial architectural forms, culminating in the cohesion in the Chavín Cult in the Early Horizon. Subsequent periods continued the alternation of less-unified periods and more politically unified horizons, although in every period there were some kingdoms or empires.

Patterns established in earlier periods continued to focus on three areas: the central and northern Peruvian coastal valleys, the central and southern Peruvian/Bolivian sierras and Altiplano, and the southern Peruvian and northern Chilean coastal deserts. Within each of these areas powerful social hierarchies developed and elite individuals ruled alongside a specialized priesthood or state shamans. Elite individuals were buried elaborately in rich tombs, sumptuously adorned and often accompanied by sacrificial victims. State cults of the dead flourished, establishing the principle of a continuously revolving cycle of life and death and the perpetuation of the dead in the living world.

The principles of state control over ordinary citizens became stronger and more elaborate, culminating in one of the two greatest empires ever established in the Americas: the Inca Empire. The chronicles and histories preserved by Spanish priests and administrators, together with archaeological discoveries, make it possible to gain a detailed picture of the way of life and beliefs of the Incas.

Left: This painted Chimú textile depicts a shaman in a trance, surrounded by snarling felines, serpents and birds.

THE NAZCA CONFEDERACY

Early Horizon Chavín was not a state religion. It brought religious unity throughout the central and northern Peruvian Andes and coast, but it was not a centralized state.

The number and variation in size and architecture of civic-ceremonial centres, and the large domestic populations of many, indicate both local rule and social organization. Specialist artisans spread and perpetuated the cult by making large quantities of portable objects adorned with Chavín symbolic art, constantly reminding the inhabitants of the towns and cities of their over-arching religion. Chavín de Huántar remained the premier pilgrimage centre, and constant trade among coastal and mountain valleys re-enforced shared beliefs.

Contemporary with later Chavín was the Paracas culture on the southern Peruvian coast. Like Chavín, Paracas was

Below: Nazca effigy jar suggesting a severed head. Ritual decapitation, widespread in Andean civilization, was a Nazca speciality.

Above: Nazca burials include collections of trophy heads and were often wrapped in textiles fringed with pictures of woven heads.

not a centralized state. The most famous Paracas feature – its Cavernas cemetery of richly adorned, carefully mummified burials – was a distinct locale serving, but physically separated from, the living town of Cerro Colorado. Close spiritual association between Paracas living and dead, demonstrated by the lavish treatment of the latter by the former, shows a cult-like relationship between religion and a loose socio-political organization. With some early Chavín influence, Paracas religion soon developed its own character, which was particularly represented by a prominent figure known as the Oculate Being.

NAZCA CITY-STATES

In the same desert coastal area as the Nazca were the Early Intermediate Period inheritors of the Paracas legacy, *c.*100BC–AD700. As with Paracas, no strong central Nazca political unity prevailed; rather there was a loose confederation of city-states in the river valleys. Ventilla, the largest Nazca site known, covered at least 200ha (495 acres) with terraced housing, walled courts and small mounds, and is thought to have been a Nazca 'capital' of one such city-state.

Ventilla was linked to its ritual counterpart, Cahuachi, by a line or 'road' across the desert. Cahuachi comprised a profusion of ceremonial kin-group mounds and associated plazas scattered over 150ha (370 acres). The mounds were built of adobe bricks modifying the tops of about 40 natural hills in mid-valley. The largest mound, known as the Great Temple, was a 30m (98ft) high modified hillock comprising six or seven terraces with adobe-brick retaining walls.

Cahuachi's location was chosen deliberately at mid-valley where, for geological reasons, the Nazca River disappears underground and re-emerges down-valley. Increasing drought in the sierra to the east intensified desert aridity and pressure for water conservation. The Ventillana-Cahuachi people constructed an elaborate system of subterranean channels to direct water into cisterns, which were reached by spiral ramps on terraces faced with river cobbles, and from which water could be drawn for irrigation.

A CITY FOR RITUAL

Cahuachi was a sacred 'city', where the citizens performed religious ceremonies and where the dead were prepared and then buried. The burials and artefacts associated with the mounds show that the entire site was a pilgrimage centre and ritual burial ground of family plots, each kin-group constructing its own mound. The focus was on ancestor worship and a pantheon of gods now nameless.

Some burials were of elite or favoured dead, while others appear to be sacrificial victims. Honoured burials were mummified and accompanied by exquisitely decorated, multicoloured woven burial coats and pottery, and sometimes by animal sacrifices. Others – men, women or children – had excrement inserted in the mouth, the skull perforated and threaded on a cord, the eyes blocked, the mouth pinned by cactus spines or the tongue removed and placed in a pouch. The meanings of such ritual practices are unknown, but the relationship between Ventilla and Cahuachi resembles and perpetuates the affiliation between the living and dead at Cerro Colorado and Cavernas.

NAZCA CRAFTS

Nazca textiles and pottery continued many Paracas traditions. They were adorned with images of the gods: half-human, half-animal – felines with long, ratcheted tails, spiders with human faces, birds, monkeys and lizards. Fringes on some textiles display rows of dangling heads or mummified

Left: A Nazca warrior or masked shaman with spear and atl-atl *(spear thrower), in a stance reminiscent of the Chavín Staff Deity.*

skulls with staring eyes, or lines of figures wearing short tunics, dancing above round-eyed deities who seem to be flying, continuing the Oculate Being tradition.

Caches of severed and trepanned skulls and dangling heads on textiles represent a Nazca trophy-head cult of sacrificial victims. Like the severed heads so prominent at Chavín de Huántar and other northern sierra and coastal sites, they demonstrate the strength of severed-head symbolism in ancient Andean religion.

RITUAL PATHWAYS

Ritual dominance of daily life was further emphasized across the desert floor by geoglyphs – the famous Nazca lines. Desert figures and patterns, resembling those on Nazca ceramics and textiles, began to be made as early as the settlements at Cahuachi, Ventilla and other sites, but increased in number and complexity as Cahuachi was abandoned. Hundreds of geometric patterns, clusters of straight lines and recognizable figures frequently cross, but individual patterns or figures are each made of a single, continuous line. Animal and other figures each comprise a single line with different beginning and end points.

Nazca geoglyphs were ritual pathways, walked for reasons no longer fully understood, but which presumably involved religious cycles. Each figure or pattern appears to have been made by and for a small group – or perhaps even an individual – each for a separate, but jointly agreed purpose and small group's use. Experiments have shown that a few people can make a geoglyph in a short time. Their number and interference with each other indicates that geoglyph-making endured over a long time period, and that individual patterns may have been for short or even a single use.

Increasing aridity of the region and disastrous earthquakes appear to have caused the Nazca to abandon Ventilla, Cahuachi and other sites. At the same time, an increase in the number and elaboration of geoglyphs seems to indicate increasing ritual, perhaps asking the gods for help.

Below: In the Nazca desert, water was channelled from underground rivers to subterranean cisterns with terraced entrances.

THE MOCHE STATE

In contrast to the loose confederacy of the Nazca, the Early Intermediate Period in the northern Peruvian coastal valleys saw the emergence of Moche state-builders.

THE FIRST TRUE STATE

Moche is arguably the first true ancient Andean state or kingdom. For about the first 600 years AD it dominated the northern coastal valleys from the Piura Valley in the north to the Harmey Valley in the south. The Lambayeque and Moche valleys are roughly in the middle of the area, a few valleys apart.

The Moche state comprised two neighbouring spheres, northern and southern, in which two related languages were spoken: Muchic from the Lambayeque Valley northwards and Quingan in the south.

Of an energetic military temperament, Moche rulers established a powerful kingdom over several hundred years through conquest and domination of the valleys

Below: The invading warrior on this Moche stirrup-spout vessel stands on a fanged-beast-prowed boat.

Above: This fierce, grimacing, half-human, half-jaguar face is that of the Moche Decapitator God at the Huaca de la Luna.

north and south of the southern sphere 'capital' at Moche in the valley of the same name. From the 4th century, Moche rulers mounted campaigns from valley to valley by sea, and many Moche pots depict narrative battle scenes of armies and pairs of warriors. A developing strong social hierarchy was reflected in burial practices.

Quingan speakers remained dominant, and Moche was the capital city for several hundred years.

HUACAS DEL SOL AND DE LA LUNA

The focuses of political and religious power in the capital were the two huge pyramidal structures known as the Huaca del Sol and the Huaca de la Luna, which reached their full sizes around AD450. Each required a massive amount of labour and was built of millions of hand-made adobe bricks. Distinctive marks on the bricks record the different labour gangs who built the platforms. The sudden appearance of similar platforms in the valleys indicates Moche conquest of the local populations.

Huaca del Sol, the seat of the Moche dynasty, comprised a four-tiered platform in the plan of a huge, stubby-armed cross

of unequal parts. Its 40m (130ft) high summit was reached by a north-side ramp. Just 500m (1,640ft) away stood the Huaca de la Luna at the foot of Cerro Blanco. La Luna was a three-tiered structure whose walls were richly decorated with friezes depicting mythological scenes and deities. The area between the two platforms, occupied by dwellings and workshops, is believed to have been the elite residential area of the city. Around this core a sprawling urban setting covered as much as 3 sq km (740 acres).

NEW CAPITALS

In the 6th century Moche power shifted north and the new 'capitals' became Sipán and, later, Pampa Grande, both in the Lambayeque Valley. Moche the capital was eventually eclipsed altogether when climatic change brought drought and the formation of a huge sand sheet that clogged the city's canal system, stifling agriculture and causing the inhabitants to emigrate. Some of Moche's inhabitants were

Above: Huaca del Sol at Moche was the largest solid, adobe-brick pyramid platform ever built in the New World.

probably responsible for the settlement of Galindo farther up the valley. Early encroachment on Moche territory by the nascent Wari state from the south-east might also have played a role in the northern power shift.

The late phase of Moche culture (Moche V) blends into the Middle Horizon, in which the Wari Empire dominated across the northern Andean Area. Nevertheless, this final, 150-year flowering of Moche culture is reflected in the rich ruler burials at Sipán, some of the few unlooted tombs of pre-Hispanic Andean civilization. They contain sumptuous burials, richly furnished with the exquisite ceramics, metalwork and textiles of Moche state artisans. These artefacts depicted scenes or represent themes similar to those on the walls, ceramics, textiles and metalwork found at Moche and other sites.

MOCHE RELIGION

Like Chavín, Moche imagery represented a potent religion, with distinctive symbols and a pantheon, albeit much derived from Chavín. It was characterized by humans and humanlike animal figures, serpents and frogs, birds (owls in particular) and sea animals (crabs and fish), and also by standardized groups and ceremonial scenes, including a coca ritual recognizable by distinctive clothing and ritual combat. Murals, friezes and vignettes on pottery depict the capture and sacrifice of 'enemies' being led with ropes around their necks, the drink offerings by subordinates to lords and gods, and persons passing through the night sky in moon-shaped boats.

Such narrative scenes offer scholars some of the earliest 'historical' sources to corroborate archaeological interpretation. Some of the characters depicted have been discovered in elite burials, being represented by their regalia. For the first time, pre-Hispanic Andean personages, if not known individuals, can be recognized.

No Moche deities are known by name. However, when the Moche state declined, the inheritors of their legacy, the Chimú, worshipped Ai Apaec, a sky/creator god, and Si, the moon goddess. They may represent religious continuity from Moche times, and were perhaps represented on the murals of the Huaca del Sol and Huaca de la Luna pyramids. The coastal region also revered a mountain god, represented by images of a feline-featured being on Moche ceramics and textiles, and on wall friezes. Even more prominent were fanged deities and a deity known as the Decapitator God, who appears frequently in the rich ceremony and ritual depicted on pots and textiles. Later Moche imagery shows a mingling with Wari style, and subtle changes in the depiction of eyes and headdress ornaments suggest the beginnings of the influence of Chimú imagery.

Left: A helmeted, kneeling Moche warrior or shaman, painted for combat, with a socketed hand, perhaps to hold a spear or war club.

THE EMPIRE OF TIWANAKU

At the same time as Chavín influence was waning in the northern sierra and coast, the peoples of the Titicaca Basin shifted their own religious fervour from the early ceremonial complex at Chiripa to several sites north of the lake. The principal site was Pukará, and the religious tradition is known as Yaya-Mama. The imagery of Yaya-Mama included universal Andean subjects – felines, serpents, lizards, birds and fish, and severed heads – but was focused especially on stone monoliths with carved male (*yaya*) and female (*mama*) figures on opposite sides.

TIWANAKU CITY

In the 1st–2nd centuries AD, however, the focus of the Titicaca Basin's political power and religious influence shifted south of the lake again as the city of Tiwanaku grew.

Below: The great Gateway of the Sun at Tiwanaku depicts a central Sun God or Staff Deity, flanked by rows of running 'angels'.

Above: The great semi-subterranean court of the Kalasasaya Temple, Tiwanaku, was one of the main ceremonial courts of the capital.

At 3,850m (12,600ft) above sea level, Tiwanaku expanded between AD200 and 500 to cover 4.5 sq km (1,100 acres) as the capital of a considerable empire within and beyond the Titicaca Basin, stretching east and west to the Bolivian lowlands, west and north-west to the Peruvian coast, and south into northern Chile. Its cultural and religious influence extended even farther, but its north-western frontiers were established where it met its chief Middle Horizon rival, the Wari Empire, at the La Raya pass south of Cuzco and in the upper reaches of the Moquegua drainage area west of Titicaca.

The core of the city formed a ceremonial-religious-civic centre, including several monumental buildings, gateways, and stone sculptures exhibiting religious motifs and gods, whose artistic symbols show particular affinities to those of Chavín, and whose influence shows the continuity of ancient religious beliefs. The civic centre was aligned east–west, confined within a moat, and surrounded by residential compounds of adobe bricks.

Tiwanaku religion was a culmination of beliefs that united the peoples of the Titicaca Basin from the Initial Period through civic-ceremonial complexes at Chiripa and Pukará. Surrounding the capital were the natural features long regarded as sacred: the waters of Lake Titicaca to the west and the snow-capped mountain peaks to the east. Tiwanaku was located in the midst of fertile land, enhanced by a sophisticated system of dikes, canals, causeways and aquaducts to irrigate crops.

The ceremonial centre was planned on a grid pattern and its structures oriented on the points of the compass. The moat around the religious precinct segregated it from the residential sections of the city, making it an artificial island, a representation of the sacred Islands of the Sun and Moon in the lake.

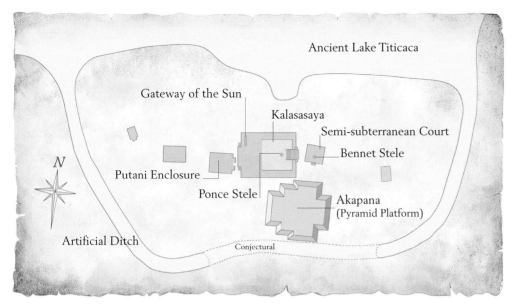

Left: Site map of Tiwanaku showing the Gateway of the Sun, the Akapana Temple, the Kalasasaya and other monuments.

A TRULY IMPERIAL CAPITAL

Construction of the major elements had begun by AD300. Stone temples, sunken courts, gateways and architraves were carved with religious imagery. Some of the buildings were probably residential palaces, but the gateways and gargantuan monumental sculptures were the focuses of public open spaces meant for civic participation in ritual and ceremony. Traces of gold pins within the stone blocks and remains of paint show that the sculptures were decorated and/or clothed in textiles.

The core of the artificial island was the Akapana Temple, a mound raised 17m (56ft) high in seven sandstone-clad tiers. Lake Titicaca and Mt Illimani are visible from the summit. Roughly T-shaped, a quadrate cruciform sunken court of andesite and sandstone slabs occupies the 50 sq m (540 sq ft) summit. Staircases climb the east and west terraces, and two staircases enter the court near rooms that might once have been priests' quarters. Subterranean stone channels drained water from the sunken court to the Tiwanaku River.

South-east of Akapana, the Pumapunku Temple T-shaped mound comprised three sandstone-slab-covered tiers, rising 5m (16ft) high and covering 150 sq m (1,615 sq ft). Its sunken summit courtyard has carved stone doorways and lintels and might have been the original location of the Gateway of the Sun.

Right: The monumental stairway of the Kalasasaya sunken court leads through a dressed-stone portal framing the Ponce Stela.

North of Akapana is the Semi-Subterranean Temple, a sunken court 28.5 × 26m (94 × 85ft), entered by a staircase on its south side. Its interior walls are adorned with carved stone heads, and at its centre stand several carved stone stelae, originally including the 'Bennett Stela' (now in La Paz). Standing 7.3m (24ft) high, it portrays a richly dressed human thought to be one of Tiwanaku's rulers or the divine ruler. He/she holds a *kero* beaker and a staff-like object, perhaps a snuff tablet.

KALASASAYA

The Kalasasaya – north of Akapana, west of the Semi-Subterranean Temple – is a low-lying rectangular platform 130 × 120m (427 × 394ft). It forms a large ceremonial precinct for public ritual, with walls made up of sandstone pillars alternating with smaller ashlar blocks. Its stairway is carved from stones set between two gigantic stone pillars.

The famous Gateway of the Sun stands at its north-west corner. It appears to comprise two monolithic stone slabs supporting a third, carved, slab across their tops, but is in fact a single huge andesite block. The crossing top face is completely carved: the central figure portrays the 'Gateway God' – a humanlike figure standing on a stepped platform resembling the tiered mounds of the sacred precinct itself. Holding staffs with its outstretched arms, it bears an obvious resemblance to the Chavín Staff Deity. It is flanked by three rows of winged figures in profile.

Within the Kalasasaya stands the giant stone Ponce Stela, 3.5m (11ft 6in) tall and visible from within the Semi-Subterranean Temple framed by the main gateway. Like the Bennett Stela, it portrays a ruler or deity, richly clothed/carved and holding a *kero* beaker and staff/snuff tablet.

Tiwanaku endured until about AD1000, waning between 900 and 1000 as climatic change brought repercussions throughout the Andean Area.

THE WARI EMPIRE

Huari was the capital city of the Wari Empire and the northern rival of Tiwanaku. Together the two empires represent the political cohesion that united the Middle Horizon for more than 500 years.

BIRTH OF AN IMPERIAL STATE

Wari dominated the central Andes and coastal valleys, and expanded into the regions of the north almost to the Ecuadorian border. One of its northernmost outposts was the city of Cajamarca in northern Peru; its southernmost was Pikillaqta near Cuzco. It met Tiwanaku expansion at the Pass of La Raya, south of Cuzco, and openly confronted Tiwanaku in the upper reaches of the Moquegua drainage area west of Titicaca, where it established a colony on the defensive summit of Cerro Baúl. This region, split between Tiwanaku in the north-west and Wari in the south-east, constituted a buffer zone between the two empires.

Below: The need for the hilltop fortress of Carangas is an example of the tense rivalry between the Wari and Tiwanaku empires.

From humble beginnings in the 3rd century AD, major constructions at Huari from the 5th century reflect the city's growing power. Its main period of imperial expansion lasted from about AD600 to 800.

The capital occupied the plateau of a mountain valley at about 2,800m (9,180ft) above sea level between the Huamanga and Huanta basins. Serving as a civic, residential and religious centre, it grew rapidly to cover more than 100ha (247 acres), then 200ha (495 acres), then 300ha (740 acres), with an additional periphery of residential suburbs occupying a further 250ha (620 acres). Its population has been variously estimated at 10,000–35,000 inhabitants.

From about 600 the Wari state spread a dominant religion, characterized by a distinctive symbolic art, through military expansion in much the same way that its coastal rival, the Moche, had expanded earlier in the northern coastal region.

Shortly before 800 there appears to have been a political crisis that caused building within the capital to slacken and cease. Simultaneously, the political

Above: The city of Huari was gradually expanded through regular additions of angular walled precincts and dressed-stone sectors.

centre and religious shrine of Pachacamac, on the central Peruvian coast, began to reassert itself and possibly even to rival Wari power. Pachacamac had flourished since later Early Intermediate Period times and had only recently been occupied by the Wari. Similarly, in its north-west provinces, the rising local power of the Sicán lords of the Lambayeque Valley challenged Wari overlordship in the late 7th century. Wari expansion ended abruptly and the capital was abandoned by AD800.

RUINS OF THE CAPITAL

The architecture of the site of Huari, although megalithic, has not survived well. Some of it approximates the grandeur of the ceremonial architecture at Tiwanaku, although more crudely. Numerous walls remain as high as

Above: The rigidly planned border fortress of Pikillaqta, the southernmost Wari town, included an extensive defensive wall.

6–12m (20–40ft). There were several rectangular compounds, and some buildings had projecting walls that supported multiple storeys.

In contrast to Tiwanaku, however, Huari's rapid expansion appears to have occurred at random, without the deliberate and preconceived planning of its competitor. The huge enclosure of Cheqo Wasi (or Huasi) included dressed stone-slab chambers. Two important temple complexes were Vegachayoq Moqo and Moraduchayoq, the latter a semi-subterranean compound resembling the one at Tiwanaku. In keeping with the comparatively frenetic pace of Huari's development, the Moraduchayoq Temple was dismantled around AD650.

SHARED RELIGION

Wari and Tiwanaku's political ambitions and military aims made them political rivals, yet they also shared symbolic religious imagery and mythology.

Much of the religious and mythological art imagery of Tiwanaku and Wari was virtually identical, which demonstrates religious continuity from the Early Horizon through the Early Intermediate Period. Despite military opposition, scholars entertain the possibility that religious missionaries from one city visited the other. It might have been that the priests were willing to set politics aside and let religious beliefs transcend such matters.

Continuity and similarities of religious symbols used in art include, in particular, the Staff Deity image, but also winged and running falcon- and condor-headed creatures – often wielding clubs – and severed trophy heads. It is reasoned that similarities in imagery show similarities in religious and cosmological belief. It seems that the gods of Chavín endured as the Staff Deity of Tiwanaku and Wari, and were responsible for human origins and for the fertility of crops and flocks. Winged beings appear both accompanying the Staff Deity and independently, and were depicted running, floating, flying or kneeling. The Staff Deity – with mask-like face, radiating head rays (sometimes ending in serpent heads), and tunic, belt and kilt – appears on pottery and architecture and might have been the prototype for the creator god Viracocha.

Despite such apparent religious unity, the focus of religious imagery in Wari differed from that in Tiwanaku. In Wari it was applied primarily to portable objects, particularly to ceramics; in Tiwanaku, however, it was concentrated on monumental stone architecture, and appeared less frequently on pottery or textiles. Thus, while Wari ceramics and textiles spread the word far and wide, Tiawanaku imagery was more confined to standing monuments at the capital and a few other sites. The ceremonial core at Tiwanaku was designed and developed as a preconceived plan, and was therefore one of public ceremony and, apparently, participation. The Wari capital of Huari, by contrast, appears to have developed more haphazardly, and religious structures were smaller and more private, implying that they were the focus of ritual of a more personal and intimate nature.

RIVALS OR ALLIES?

Given these similarities and differences, the exact nature of the relationship between the two kingdoms or empires remains enigmatic. The two empires seemed to keep each other at arms' length, but they may have exchanged political and religious ambassadors to each other's capital city. Nevertheless, it is clear that religious concepts and imagery prevailed through the politically fragmented Early Intermediate Period as well as within the more unified imperial Middle Horizon.

Below: Although political rivals, Wari and Tiwanaku shared a religion, here represented by a kero *drinking cup with a serpentine motif.*

THE KINGDOM OF CHIMÚ

Adverse climate change and early Wari incursions in the early Middle Horizon pushed late Moche power north to the Lambayeque Valley. A new capital was established at Pampa Grande, which endured for about 150 years. Moche religious belief also changed, dropping much of the old pantheon and focusing on maritime imagery – a precursor to the Chimú symbols that followed in the Late Intermediate Period.

PAMPA GRANDE

This new capital covered some 6 sq km (1,485 acres). Its most imposing structure, Huaca Fortaleza, appears to have served a function similar to the Huaca del Sol at Moche. Rising 38m (125ft) above the valley floor, its summit was reached by a 290m (950ft) ramp. At the top, columns supported the roofs of a complex of rooms, one containing a mural

Below: The founders of the Chimú dynasty arrived from the sea, as demonstrated by this Chimú stirrup-spouted burnished pot.

showing feline beings. Huaca Fortaleza was probably the elite sector of the city, with lower-class residences spread around it.

Like Moche, Pampa Grande was abandoned abruptly, owing to agricultural disaster caused by an El Niño weather event and the continued expansion of the Wari Empire from the south. Fierce internal unrest may also have occurred, for archaeological evidence has revealed intense destructive fires in the centre of the city, so hot that adobe mud bricks of the Huaca Fortaleza were fired.

THE SICÁN LORDS

The inheritors of the late Moche flourishing in the Lambayeque Valley were the Sicán Lords. For centuries overshadowed by the power of the Wari Empire, they emerged as a local power and made rich burials from the 9th to the 14th centuries at Batán Grande as Wari power waned.

The Sicán Lords were one of many local resurgences repulsing Wari and Tiwanaku power.

Above: Detail of a painted cotton Chimú textile of a shaman or chieftain flanked by two felines and wielding an axe.

After Pampa Grande and Batán Grande, northern coastal power shifted again, back south to the Moche Valley, where the rise of the Kingdom of Chimú (or Chimor) eclipsed Sicán power.

THE RISE OF THE CHIMÚ

The Chimú established their capital across the Moche River at Chan Chan, in the shadows of Moche Huacas del Sol and de la Luna.

Chimú was the largest Andean Area empire before the Incas. Over 400 years, Chimú lords subdued the northern coastal and inland valleys, eventually controlling two-thirds of the irrigated land along the desert coast. With Chimú begin obscure historical accounts, although these are filtered through Inca interpretations.

The Chimú came from outside the valley and their history seems to hark back to a legendary conqueror called Naymlap, possibly the Moche king who invaded the Lambayeque Valley. Naymlap's eldest son, Cium, established a dynasty of 12 rulers, each of whom kept the green stone statue-idol of Yampallec set up by Naymlap. The final ruler, Fempellec, wanted to remove the

idol but was thwarted by 'the devil', and the priests, who abducted Fempellec, threw him into the ocean and ended the dynasty.

Two sources describe the foundation of Chimú by a conqueror from the sea (possibly from Lambayeque), variously called Chimu Capac or Taycanamu. A dynasty of 12 rulers might correspond to the Chimú compounds at Chan Chan, although the Chimú king list recorded by the Incas names only ten kings.

CITY OF THE LIVING AND DEAD

Chan Chan was founded about AD1000 and was conquered by Inca Tupac Yupanqui in the 1470s. Its core was an inner city of the living and the dead, a complex of individual compounds (called *ciudadelas*) covering 6 sq km (1,480 acres). Surrounding residential and industrial suburbs covered another 14 sq km (3,460 acres). There are ten compounds (although different interpreters propose

Below: A wooden figure with a mud-plaster face mask. This would have stood in a niche at the entrance to a ciudadela *compound.*

between nine and twelve). Nine compounds have a truncated pyramid in the southeast corner, entered from above through a court to a suite of cells and a larger room thought to have housed the mummified body of a king.

Each *ciudadela*, a rectangle oriented north–south, comprised a miniature city enclosed within thick poured-adobe mud walls up to 9m (30ft) high, most with a single, northern entrance. Niches on either side of the entrances held painted wooden human figures as guards. Established as the court of the ruler, each *ciudadela* formed the residence of the reigning king, his officials and retainers, and became a sealed city of the dead after his death. Inner walls divided the compounds into courtyards surrounded by houses, storerooms, U-shaped structures (*audiencias*) and walled-in wells. Resident retainers perpetuated a cult of each deceased king. Along the south walls of the compounds ramps led up to burial platforms for each royal family.

The U-shaped structures appear to reflect recognition of and reverence for ancient U-shaped ceremonial complexes of the area. Burials were placed in and near them and their shape may represent a 'cosmic niche'. Association with store rooms suggests that they were also for redistribution, part of a tightly controlled

Above: The core of the Chimú capital at Chan Chan comprised ciudadela *compounds, each devoted to the cult of a deceased king.*

system for the collection and distribution of wealth, foods and commodities among the nobility and general populace, according to social rank.

Five monumental adobe mounds at Chan Chan might have been temple platforms, although they have been so damaged by treasure seekers that it is not possible to be sure of their function. One platform, however, contained more than 200 bodies, including young women who might have been sacrificed to accompany a Chimú king into the afterlife.

Generally, Chimú imagery found at Chan Chan and elsewhere was a merging of Moche and Wari styles. Chimú ritual architecture reveals Wari influence in fanged deities, jaguars, jaguar-humans and serpents alongside marine imagery. The *ciudadela* walls were carved with repetitious friezes of geometric patterns, images of birds and marine animals, and of the double-headed rainbow-serpent being, the last apparently associated with Si, the moon goddess, one of the few Chimú deities that we know by name. Ai Apaec was the sky/creator god who was very ancient to this region, and Ni, the sea god, reflects northern coastal marine importance.

THE INCA EMPIRE

The Inca Empire was the largest political unity ever created in the New World. It was as large and powerful as many contemporary states in Europe.

DESTINED TO RULE

The foundation of the empire, or the early stages of the Inca state, is steeped in the legendary journey of a band of brothers and sisters. Modern scholars regard the tale as a mythical hero-legend, especially in its mystical implications of underground journeys and re-emergence from the earth. The archaeological and historical evidence shows that the Incas arose in the Cuzco Valley as one among many local 'tribes' or nations – town- or city-states – all of which were of long-standing native origin.

The arrival of influential individuals from outside, however, may have some basis in fact as a group of assertive individuals who were able to persuade the Incas of their rulership abilities and legitimacy, and to lead them on a path towards domination of their rivals in the valley. Once the Incas had overcome their neighbours, their rulers embarked on a dedicated programme of conquest beyond the valley. From Pachacuti Inca Yupanqui, who overcame the Incas' principal rivals, the Chancas, in 1438, the conquest of vast territories in all directions from Cuzco was what drove the empire.

The Incas believed in their destiny, and therefore in their right, to rule. They considered themselves to be the pinnacle of cyclical development in the world – politically, religiously and socially. They and their systems were not the culmination of, but the final solution to a predetermined course of history that would end sometime in the future by the empire's descent into chaos and by the beginning of, or more accurately, the 'turning over', of the cycle and the start of a new 'Sun' or age.

Above: In addition to the axe-spear, a favourite Inca weapon was the stone- or iron-headed war club.

RECORDING HISTORY

The Incas recorded their history orally and through the use of bundles of knotted string called *quipus*. State history was kept by imperial officials called *amautas* (court historians) and *quipucamayoqs* (knot-makers). Using *quipus* as an *aide-mémoire*, they were responsible for keeping the state histories alive through detailed oral history and regular recital. They kept, and on official state occasions reminded the populace of, the official history of the foundation and growth of Cuzco and of the Inca conquests. The early history was grounded in the story of the founder brother-sister pairs and their legendary journey, and of the exploits of early leaders and state heroes. The *amautas* also memorized and recited the royal genealogy, a formidable task, as Inca rulers had several wives and many children, and the royal household grew to include hundreds of members.

As the empire was expanded through conquest, the *amautas* were tasked with adding to the official history of the state, and with reconciling the events and situation 'on the ground' with Inca concepts and their perception of the cycle. To do this, much of their new subjects'

Below: Map of Cuzco with an inset map showing how the city plan was in the shape of a crouching puma.

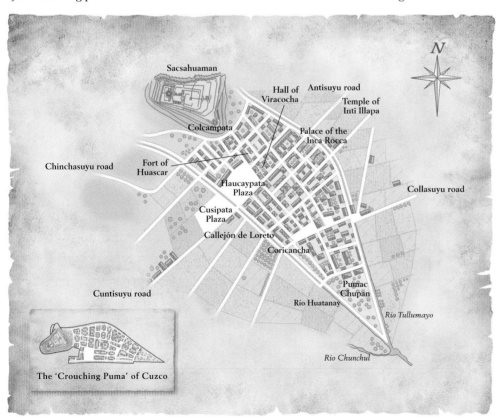

Sacsahuaman

Hall of Viracocha
Antisuyu road
Temple of Inti Illapa

Colcampata
Palace of the Inca Rocca

Chinchasuyu road
Fort of Huascar

Collasuyu road

Haucaypata Plaza

Cusipata Plaza

Callejón de Loreto

Coricancha

Cuntisuyu road

Pumac Chupán

Río Huatanay

Río Tullumayo

Río Chunchul

The 'Crouching Puma' of Cuzco

Above: The circular tower and surrounding walls of Sacsahuaman at Cuzco may represent the sun as the central temple to Inti.

myths, legends, histories, dynastic ties and religious tenets were recast and/or incorporated into the Inca story, as if they had been part of the history in the first place. This official version was particularly important in the establishment of Inti the sun as the supreme being and object of official state worship, which had to be construed in such a manner that it was acceptable to conquered peoples who harboured their own local deities, most of whom were long-standing and entrenched.

Paralleling the obscurity of the early stages of the Inca version of history, the archaeological record leaves scholars with little evidence of pre-Inca Cuzco. The capital has been continuously occupied since Inca times, especially since being substantially rebuilt by Pachacuti Inca Yupanqui and his successors through the 15th and early 16th centuries. As a result, many Inca structures form the foundations for Spanish Colonial and later buildings, and therefore it is not known what lies beneath. No recognizably distinct Inca

architectural style can be identified with any of the pre-Pachacuti Inca emperors. It is not certain if the earliest Inca rulers ruled from Cuzco, co-existed with other local rulers or even lived in Cuzco.

SUBJUGATION PROBLEMS

Inca subjugation was through armed conquest, but such was the success and perceived inevitability of Inca rule that many tribes gave them little resistance. Nevertheless, resentment among peoples at the extremes of the empire led to frequent truculence, even open revolt, and peoples beyond the imperial borders raided into the fringes, sometimes with local collusion.

Tribes of the eastern tropical forests were the only group that successfully resisted conquest. The Incas, a mountain people, were psychologically attuned to distance vistas and lines of sight, and to a landscape of rugged variation. In attempting conquest into the rainforests flanking the eastern Cordillera, therefore, they were simply out of their element. Their commanders were lost; their points of reference were lost. They were up against an illusive foe that fought not *en masse* in open warfare but by stealth from

protected cover. Yet the Incas admired tropical forest warriors and used their bowmen in the imperial army. Similarly, animals of the rainforest, especially the jaguar, were revered for their power, strength and cunning.

Below: A kero or painted wooden drinking cup showing an Inca warrior in a feather headdress and holding a spear.

POLITICS OF EMPIRE

The Inca Empire was divided into four unequal quarters, radiating from Cuzco. The quarters were known as *suyus* and formed Tahuantinsuyu – the 'four united parts' or 'four parts together'. The word itself is recorded only in later Spanish colonial sources, and it is not known if the Incas actually used the word themselves in this context. The term might have been first used around 1570 by Titu Cusi Yupanqui, the leader in Vilcabamba of an Inca revolt against Spanish rule. Alternatively, use of the term might have been an inflation of a more restricted use for the organization of the *ceque* shrines around Cuzco, first located by the Spanish magistrate Polo de Ondegardo.

Antisuyu, the smallest part, comprised the eastern Andean slopes and tropical forests north-east of Cuzco; Collasuyu, the largest part, stretched south-east from Cuzco, comprising southern Peru, the Titicaca Basin, western Bolivia, north-western Argentina and northern Chile; Chinchasuyu comprised the north-west

Above: A collca *(storehouse) built in traditional Inca vernacular style at Ollantatamba in the Urubamba Valley.*

Below: Inca accountants keep records on a quipu *of the collection of produce into store-houses for distribution among subject peoples.*

region of western Peru and Ecuador; and Cuntisuyu comprised south-western Peru to the coast. The common point of the four *suyus* was the Coricancha Temple, the most sacred precinct in Cuzco. From this point radiated real and sighted sacred lines and routes known as *ceques*.

INCA STATE ORGANIZATION

The Inca state was rooted in the past, following a long line of political and social arrangements that had developed in the Andean Area from early times. Much of Inca state organization owed a debt to the Middle Horizon and Late Intermediate Period empires of the Wari, Tiwanaku and Chimú.

The foundation of Inca strength, and often the basis of others' capitulation, was the ancient Andean practice of the formalized exchange of goods and ideas between highlands and lowlands –

between mountain and coast, Altiplano and desert. The Wari and Tiwanaki states had established regional administrative centres, formalized systems of exchange, roads and way-stations, and a sponsored state cult. In the farther-flung regions of the Inca Empire, administrative centres often had to be created from scratch if nothing lingered there from earlier times.

KEEPING CONTROL

The Inca appointed provincial governors (*tocoyrikoqs*) over conquered nations and city-states. Local chiefs (*curakas*) were incorporated into the system by being retained alongside the *tocoyrikoqs*, and together the pair administered the regional *mit'a*, or labour tax. Inca state tax was of three types: agricultural, *mit'a* and a textile tax. Agricultural taxes were extracted from the produce of *ayllu* kinship-owned land, imperial land and general communal land regulated by the *curakas*; it involved the labour of men and women. The *mit'a* tax was extracted only from able-bodied men. The textile tax was paid mainly as cloth woven by women, but also included fibre cordage and rope made by men.

Inca state control was maintained in a number of ways. In addition to military force, they practised various forms of removal and hostage holding.

One form was the deliberate transfer of whole or portions of populations within the empire. Known as *mitamaqs*, the practice was used to exercise demographic and social control, and to sustain an even economy. Local *curakas* were removed with their people. By shifting large groups of people around within the empire, the Incas could redistribute labour and the commodities grown and produced by different groups and mix peoples' ideas of geographic identity and religious/mythological concepts. One prominent example was Inca Tupac Yupanqui's relocation of thousands of individuals from several ethnic groups to the Cochabamba Valley (Bolivia) in Collasuyu, where the Inca wanted to increase coca production.

Relocating loyal peoples to frontier provinces helped to secure the imperial borders against hostile outsiders. Conversely, relocating rebellious groups served to break up and disperse potential seditious peoples within the empire. An example was the relocation of the Cañari people of Chinchasuyu, after defeating them in battle, to the Yucay Valley near Cuzco. The Cañari became such loyal servants that the Inca granted them the status of Incas-by-privilege. The practice undoubtedly had a significant impact in creating a state religion, and the result authorized the Incas to rule as a chosen people, whose semi-divine ruler was sanctioned by the creator god Viracocha.

FRAGILE EMPIRE

Rapid expansion of the Inca Empire in the 15th century brought together a multitude of local ethnic groups, large and small city-states and regional political confederations, and many languages, customs and local religious practices. The rapidity and incompleteness of expansion, as well as the disruption caused by the Spaniards, who first arrived in 1502, probably undermined state stability and contributed to a lack of cohesion. The variety of ethnic groups

Above: Communications in the empire were maintained by a system of trunk roads from Cuzco and linking roads to provincial towns.

contributed to local loyalty, and Inca political practices were designed more for securing state revenue and begrudging state loyalty by one form of coercion or another than for genuine national unity. Even the Inca practice of relocation kept people within their ethnic units rather than integrating nationalities.

SOCIAL ORGANIZATION

The general populace of the empire was known as the *hatun-runa* ('great populace'), the bulk of which were farmers or herders. Within the empire, however, the people were subdivided into units by age, occupation and kinship groups.

INCA SOCIAL UNITS

The Inca administration organized the empire into a hierarchy of units comprising up to 10,000 individuals. The smallest unit was ten individuals, which was overseen by a foreman. Ten such units were overseen by a 'chief of 100'. A regular census was taken and monitored, and any necessary reorganization carried out accordingly.

The populace was classified into a number of age groups according to the types of work each was expected to do. For example, many males, especially single males, between the ages of 25 and 50 were expected to serve in the army. Others were expected to work the land,

Below: On the Altiplano *of Collasuyu the Incas used raised and irrigated fields to feed the growing population of the empire.*

including work on imperial lands to fulfil the labour tax. Census records were kept on *quipus* by special officials who were known as *runaquipu-camayoc* ('people-*quipu*-specialists').

Family lineages or kinship groups were organized into *ayllus*. An *ayllu* comprised the group of related individuals, their property, and a social charter of recognized mutual and collective obligation among the members.

THE SAPA INCA AND *PANACAS*

The Inca ruler was known as Sapa Inca – 'sole' or 'unique' Inca. Each Sapa Inca was regarded as the direct descendant of the founder-brother Manco Capac, and simultaneously the manifestation of the sun – Inti – on Earth. His presence brought light and warmth to make the world habitable. Such belief perpetuated the early Andean melding of politics and religion: the Sapa Inca was not only the supreme ruler, but also the supreme god on Earth, presented in human manifestation.

The ruling Sapa Inca had many wives, one of whom was his principal wife. Maternal descent was of equal, if not

Above: Inca potato and quinoa planting, depicted by Guaman Poma de Ayala in his Nueva Crónica y Buen Gobierno, *c.1613.*

dominant, importance in Inca succession to the throne. The royal household comprised several *ayllus*, called *panacas*. Each *panaca* was divided into two halves – termed *hanan* (upper) and *hurin* (lower). A principal responsibility of the *panaca* was the care of the mummy of the deceased Sapa Inca. Thus, in theory, a new *panaca* was formed at the death of each emperor. Within the Cuzco Valley, peoples conquered in the early expansion of the empire were given special benefits and called 'Incas-by-privilege'.

SECURING GOODS AND LOYALTY

Each *ayllu* owed *mit'a* service to the royal household, and the produce of their labour belonged to the state or, ultimately, to the Sapa Inca. *Mit'a* labour could take the form of working royal agricultural lands, tending royal llama flocks or producing quotas of goods such as ceramics, metalwork or textiles in state installations. It could even involve working as keepers and clerks in the *collcas* (royal warehouses) into which the produce provided by *mit'a* labour was collected.

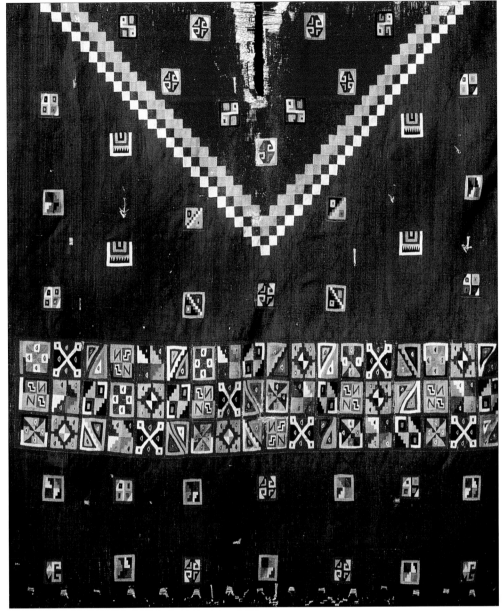

Above: The production of exquisite textiles for the rulers and nobles, and for the army, was an Inca state-sponsored industry.

bureaucracy, thus encouraging through them the loyalty of subject peoples. So impressed were the Incas with the Chimú that they took their lords back to Cuzco along with an entourage of their best gold- and silversmiths.

CHOSEN WOMEN

Another detached group within Inca society comprised the *acllas* (literally 'to choose'): 'chosen women' picked to serve in the state cults, particularly those of the sun and of the moon. Usually chosen when they were prepubescent girls so that they could be trained for the position, *acllas* also often became secondary wives and were used in imperial marriage alliances. *Acllas* were housed in special buildings called *acllahuasi*. The principal one was in Cuzco, but *acllahuasi* were also located in many provincial administrative centres. The fact that these chosen women were removed permanently from their homelands at an early age meant that they became so incorporated into the Inca system that they retained little attachment to their provincial roots and were therefore loyal to the empire.

Below: This Inca storehouse is within walled compounds among terraced fields, making maximum use of available growing surfaces.

Collca storehouses were distributed throughout the provinces. In them were stored agricultural produce, especially maize, and industrial products – surpluses of food, ceramics and other manufactured goods, and textiles for redistribution. In return for organizing and providing *mit'a* labour, the *curakas* received payment in luxury items from the Sapa Inca: fine textiles, metalwork and *chicha*, the beer made from fermented maize. It has been suggested that one reason behind continued Inca expansion was the need to secure more *mit'a* labour to meet the state's pact with the *curakas*, clearly a system that perpetuated itself.

The Sapa Inca's court also included selected retainers known as *yanacona*. These individuals were given various positions within the empire, including appointments at local-level governorships, whose loyalty to court could be relied on because they had no direct ties to the native population.

Members of the local elite, or the sons and daughters thereof, were taken to Cuzco as hostages. They were treated well, but were nonetheless held under house arrest. Likewise, the sacred objects of conquered peoples were removed to Cuzco to be held for safe-keeping as a means of ensuring loyalty – a practice used by the Wari and the Tiwanaku and continued by the Incas. Another practice was to train the sons of local chiefs to fill positions in the lower ranks of Inca

GLOSSARY

View of Machu Picchu from the Sun Gate.

acllas chosen women, picked to serve in the state cult of Inti
acllahuasi special buildings where *acllas* were housed
amarus mythical serpent-dragons
amautas also *harahuicus* Inca record-keepers
andones hillside terraces
apacheta special type of *huaca* – a stone cairn on a mountain pass or at a crossroads
apu sacred deity who lives on a mountain top, or can be the mountain top itself
aridenes cultivation terraces
atl-atl spear thrower
auca treasonous enemy of the state
audiencias small divisions within Chan Chan *ciudadela*
ayar legendary ancestors of the Incas
ayllu a kinship group or division with mutual obligations to other *ayllus*
ayni the principle that governed cyclicity
capacocha specially selected sacrificial victim

ceque sighting line or sacred pathway leading from Cuzco
chachapuma puma-headed person
chicha beer made from maize
chullpa tower where the Colla people put mummified remains, and into which more could be added
ciudadela Chimú walled compound at Chan Chan
collca storehouse
curaca leader/official
curandero person skilled in the use of herbs and potions
hanan upper
huaca a sacred place. It can be a natural wonder, man-made or modified natural feature
huaca adatorio sanctuary or temple
huaca sepultura burial place of the most important deceased individuals
huanca stone(s) regarded as the petrified ancestor of a people or *apu*
huauques man-made statues – doubles – made in the image of the ruling Sapa Incas and other chiefs and nobles during their lifetimes
hurin lower
idolatrías Spanish Colonial documents written as reports of the Spaniards' investigations of idolatrous practices among the native peoples
inqa (also *inqaychu*, *conopa* or *illa*) small stones that either resemble animals or plants or have been

carved to do so, believed to be gifts from mountain *apus*
intihuatana a 'hitching post of the sun' – special *huaca* of Inti
kalanka rectangular hall used for public functions
kancha a residential building
kero a drinking cup, especially for *chicha*, made from wood, pottery, gold or silver
mallquis mummified founding ancestor, Inca emperor or local leader
mama female
mit'a labour service/tax
mitamaes peoples redistributed within an empire
mitamaq the redistribution of people
montaña forested slopes of the Andes
moza commoner/outsider
napa miniature llama figurine
pacarina the place of origin, the place from which one's ancestors (one's tribe, nation or *ayllu* kinship group) emerged

Approaching ruins of Sayaqmarka.

pachacuti a turning over/revolution/a cycle of the world
pampa vast prairie in South America south of the Amazon
panaca kinship group; the royal panaca was the Inca *ayars*
plazas hundidas plazas or sunken courts
puna sierra basin or a valley
qhaqha person or animal that has been killed by lightning
quipu system of knotted bundles of string of different colours, this was used for recording information
quipucamayoqs knot-makers (i.e. makers and keepers of *quipus*)
runakuna Inca descendants who wear traditional clothing made from llama-wool
runaquipu-camayoc a census recorder
suyu quarter of the Inca Empire
tambo a way-station, which was used to accommodate pilgrims
tocoyrikoq provincial governor
topacusi a golden cup or vessel
tumbaga amalgamated precious metals
tumi sharp crescent-shaped knife typically used for ritual bloodletting or decapitation
wasi covered chamber
yanacona a selected court retainer
yaya male

INDEX

Black llamas were considered sacred.

A
agriculture 48, 65, 78, 100
Ai Apaec 60, 89, 111, 117
Akapana 113
alpacas 43, 45, 98
Altiplano 44–5
amautas 14, 118
Antisuyu 28–9, 48–9, 105, 120
apachetas 57, 60
apu 60, 100–1
apus 56
aqueducts 44, 47, 59, 84, 112
archaeology 18–19, 20–21
Archaic Period 22–3
Aspero 77, 94–5
Atacama Desert 46, 50
atl-atl 109
Ayar Uchu 57
ayars 32
ayllu 14, 31, 32, 57, 60, 65, 121, 122
Azángaros 105
Aztecs 13, 36

B
Bandurria 94
Batán Grande 116

C
Cahuachi 59, 84, 108–9
Cajamarca 25, 37, 38, 56, 114
Canas 105
Capac Raymi 71
Caral 95
Cardál 79, 101
Casma Valley 85, 101
Cavernas 82, 108–9
ceque lines 29, 64–5
Cerro Blanco 85, 110
Cerro Colorado 82 108, 109
Cerro Sechín 73, 79, 100–1
Chachapoyas 88, 105
Chan Chan 21, 56, 89, 116–17
Chancas 33, 56, 90, 104–5, 118
Chancay textiles 77
Chavín
  art 49, 83, 103, 108
  cult 81, 83, 103, 112–3
Chavín de Huántar 20–1, 58, 80–1, 101, 102–3, 108
Chichausuyu 28, 29
Chimú 22
  deities 60, 89, 117
  fortresses 104
  kingdom 98–9, 90, 105, 116
  kings 117
  textile 107, 116
Chimú Capac 117
Chinchaysuyu 30, 33, 105, 120–1
Chinchorros 75, 82, 97
Chiriguanas 105
Chiripa 89, 82–3, 87, 112
Chunchos 49, 105
ciudadellas 117
climate zones 46, 61
Colla 33, 105
Collasuyu 28, 33, 49, 120–1, 122
Columbus, Christopher 12
Coricancha 18, 29, 64–5, 120
cotton 46, 48, 76–7, 78, 98–9
Cotton Preceramic Period 22–3, 76–7
creation stories 14, 57
crops 45, 46, 66, 71, 78, 98, 122
Cuntisuyu 28, 33, 105, 120
curacas 120–1, 123
Cuzco 28, 30–31, 32

D
De Almagro, Diego 13, 38–9
De Soto, Hernando 37, 38
decapitation 129, 162, 181
Decapitator God 85
dialects 16
domestication 45, 76

E
Early Horizon 24, 80–3
Early Intermediate Period 24, 84–5
earthquakes 50–1, 61, 109
El Paraíso 77, 79, 94–5, 98, 100–1
Empire of the Sun 26–7
exchange of goods 66, 98
explorers, early 18–19

F
farming 53, 66
feather workers 67
Fempellec 88, 116–17

Huayna Picchu overlooking Machu Picchu.

Depiction of ancestor worship.

fishing 78
Formative Period 22–3, 76–7
four quarters of the empire 28–29, 64–5, 90, 120

G
Galindo 111
Garagay 79, 101
Gateway of the Sun 19, 103, 112–13
Guitarrero Cave 75, 76
Guzmango 105

H
hallucinogenic plants 67
  coca 48–9, 53, 109
Hanan Pacha 68–9
Hatun Colla 104
hatun-runa 122
high altitude, effects of 50
Horca del Inca 71
hostages 91, 123
Huaca de la Luna 60, 85, 110–11, 116
Huaca de los Idolos 95
Huaca de los Reyes 79, 101
Huaca de los Sacrificios 95
Huaca del Sol 85, 110–11, 116
Huaca Fortaleza 85, 116
Huaca Prieta 77, 94

External view of Sacsahuaman.

huacas 56–7
Huacaypata Plaza 28, 65
Huanca of Chinchaysuyu 105
Huancavilcas 105
Huánuco Pampa 19, 21, 30
  battle of 34, 35
Huari 19, 86, 87, 114–15
Huarochirí 105
Huayna Capac 13, 28, 33, 34, 36, 49, 56, 90–1, 104–5
Huaynuna 94, 95
Hurin Pacha 69
Huyna Capac 21

I
Inca
  architecture 61
  calendar 65, 69, 70
  civil war 13, 34–5, 36
  cosmology 68
  creation history 16
  Empire 16, 90, 118–19
  farmers 67
  potato 122
  rule 105
  society 64, 65
  state religion 33
  statecraft 33
  succession 122
  Trail 65

Inca Atahualpa 12, 13, 33, 34–7, 38–9, 56, 91
Inca Huáscar 13, 33, 34–5, 36–7, 58, 56, 71, 91
Inca Roca 32, 49
Inca Pachacuti Yupanqui 29, 32–3, 49, 56, 59, 61, 64, 90, 104, 90–1, 105, 118, 119
Inca Tupac Yupanqui 30, 33, 35, 49, 56, 91, 105, 117, 121
Inca Urco 33
Inca Viracocha 33, 49, 104
Initial Period 23, 78–9
Inti 29, 119, 122
Inti Raymi 71
irrigation 31, 43, 44, 46, 47, 53, 65, 66, 78, 99, 100–1, 108, 112
Island of the Moon 112
Island of the Sun 112

J
jaguars 48

K
Kai Pacha 68
Kalasasaya 86, 103, 113
Karwa 24
kero 113, 115, 119
Kotosh 96–7

Inca armies subdued the empire.

A female representation of the staff of Deity.

L
La Florida 79, 101
La Galgada 77, 79, 96–7, 100–1
La Paloma 75
Lake Titicaca 42, 44–5, 58–9, 82, 87, 112–13
Lambayeque 21, 85, 110, 114, 116–17
landscape 40–53
language 15, 16, 33, 88–9
Lanzón Stone 80–1, 102–3
Late Horizon 25, 90–1
Late Intermediate Period 25, 88–9
Lima 19
Lithic 23, 74
llama 42, 43, 45, 48, 53, 66, 76, 78, 96, 99
Los Morteros 94
Lupaqa 33
Lupaqas of Chucuito 104

M
Machu Picchu 21
Mañaris 105
Manco Capac 29, 32, 39, 49, 90, 122
Manosuyu 105
Manta 105
mathematics 17
mausoleums 56
Mayta Capac 33
meat 98

Mesoamerica 13
metals 49
Middle Horizon 24, 86–7
migration 66, 74, 99
Milky Way 29, 55, 58, 64, 68–9, 70–1, 79, 101
Minchançaman 33, 105
mitamaes 14
mitamaqs 121
Moche
  burials 16, 21
  culture 111
  dynasty 24
  pottery 60, 99
  State 85, 110–11
  textiles 60
  Valley 21, 1101
Mochica 16
Monte Verde 75
Moquegua 114
Moraduchayoq 115
Mosna Valley 80
Moxeke 79, 101
Moxeke-Pampa de los Llamas 79
Muchic 110
mummies 82–3, 97, 122

N
national taxation 33
Naymlap 88, 89, 116
Nazca 84
  burials 108
  cemeteries 85

The sentry post of Runkuaqay.

Cuzco from Sacsahuaman.

confederacy 108–09
culture 62, 85
geoglyphs 59, 62–3,
    84–5, 109
mummies 84, 109
pottery 85, 109
settlements 84
textiles 84
Nemterequeteba 205
Ni 89, 117
Ninancuyuchi 34–5

O
Oculate Being 82–3,
    108–9
Opataris 105
oral history 118
Otavalos 105

P
Pacaje, 105
Pacha Mama 68, 78, 80,
    82, 101
Pachacamac (city) 19, 86,
    88, 114
Pachacamac (deity) 61, 89
Pachamachay 23
Paititi 105
Palaeoindian 19, 23, 75
pampa 62
Pampa Grande 85, 110,
    116
panaca 35, 64, 122
Paracas 21, 83, 109

culture 108
    mummies 82–3
    necropolis 84
    pottery 83
Paracas Peninsula 82
Paraíso Tradition 79
Paria 31
Pariacaca 57
pastoralism 66, 100
Paucarcollas 105
Piedra Parada 94–5
Pifos 105
Pikillaqta 87, 88, 114–15
Pikimachay Cave 74
pilgrimage 60
Pilillacta 24
Pinahua Capac 104
Piura Valley 110
Pizarro, Francisco 12–13,
    24, 36–7, 38–9, 90–1
Pizarro, Hernando 37,
    38–9
place names 17
plants 23
platform mounds 96, 100
platforms, pyramidal 87
collca (Pleiades) 71, 129
Ponce Stela 113
pottery 16, 78, 84
Preceramic Period 23,
    76–7
processional routes 64
Pucca Pukará 32
Pukará 82–3, 112

Inca surveyors engineered a road system.

ceramics 83
cult 83
culture 83
Pumapunku 113
Puná 105
Puruchuco 17
Pururaucas 56, 57

Q
Qenqo 56
Quecuamaran 16
Quingan 110
quipu 14, 16, 17
quipucamayoqs 14, 15,
    118
quipus 118, 122
Quito 28, 33, 39, 105

R
Raimondi Stela 81, 103
rainfall 50, 53, 76, 101
record-keepers 67
redistribution of produce
    67
Rio Seco 94
ritual
    goods 99
    objects 67
    ploughing 65
roads 29, 31, 64, 121
royal historians 67
royal panacas 65
Runa Simi 16
runaquipu-camayoc 122

S
sacrifice
    animal 109
    capacocha 21, 64
    human 109
Sacsahuaman 11, 28, 33,
    105, 119
Salinas de Chao 77, 94–5
Sechín Alto 21, 79, 101
Sechín Bajo 79
Sechín-Casma Valley 101
Sechura Desert 46, 85
severed heads 109
Si 89, 111, 117

Taking a mummy to the mausoleum.

Sicán culture 25, 89, 114,
    116
Sinchi Roca 32
Sipán 21, 85, 110–11
smallpox 13, 25
Spanish
    chroniclers 14–15
    Conquest 36
    conquistadors 12–13, 14,
        18, 21, 37
    Inquisition 39
Staff Deity 80–1, 87,
    115
sunken courts 77, 79,
    86–7, 96–7, 100–1,
    102
Supe 77
Supe-Aspero Tradition
    94

Remains of the Muyu Marca Tower.

T
Tahuantinsuyu 28
Tambo Colorado 30–1
Tambo Grande 37
taxation 33, 122
   mit'a 14, 31, 53, 91, 99, 121, 122–3
   of textiles 45, 121
Taycanamu 89, 117
Tello Obelisk 81, 103
Temple of the Crossed Hands 76
Temple of the Cult of Chavín 93
terracing, agricultural 31, 43, 44, 46, 51, 78, 99
textile ideograms 17
textile workers 67
Titu Cusi Yupanqui 120

Tiwanaku Empire 86–7, 88, 112–13
tobacco 49, 99
Tocay Capac 104
trade 52–3, 66
Tres Ventanas Cave 76
trophy heads 83, 109
Tumbes 13, 36

U
Uku Pacha 68–9
U-shaped
   ceremonial centres 79, 80–1, 95, 100–2, 117
   temple structures 61, 102
ushnu stone 65

V
Valdivia Tradition 94
Valverde, Father 38

Vegachayoq Moqo 115
Ventilla 84, 108–09
Ventillana-Cahuachi people 108
Viracocha 28, 29, 33, 68, 87, 89, 115, 121
volcanic activity 51, 61

W
Wari Empire 86-7, 111, 114–15
   break-up of 88
water 58–9, 65
   cisterns 47, 59
   holy 58
   springs 59
weather patterns 42, 50, 58
   El Niño 51, 58, 79, 116
wool 43, 45, 78, 98–9

worship
   of ancestors 82, 109
   of mountains 63
   of ruler 8

Y
Yampallec 116
Yaya-Mama 112
Yupanqui Capac 32–3, 90

Scene from Sayaqmarka.

PICTURE ACKNOWLEDGEMENTS

The Ancient Art and Architecture Collection: 6bl, 23tl, 23br, 35bl, 63bl, 78, 80bl, 88bl, 91bm, 109tl, 117tr.
The Art Archive: /Archaeological Museum, Lima/Dagli Orti: 23tm, 76, 82, 83tm, /Biblioteca Nazionale Marciana, Venice/Dagli Orti: 37tl, /Dagli Orti: 24tr, 42tr, 58bl, 72–3, 78bl, 86, 92–93, 100bl, 103tr, 112bl, /Musee du Chateau de Versailles/Dagli Orti: 13tr, /Museo Ciudad, Mexico/Dagli Orti: 18tr, /Museo del Oro, Lima/Dagli Orti: 111bm, /Museo Nacional Tiahuanacu, La Paz, Bolivia/Dagli Orti: 22ml, 118tr, /Museo Pedro

de Osma, Lima/Mireille Vautier: 25tr, 33tr, 104tr, /Navy Historical Service, Vincennes, France/Dagli Orti: 18bl, /Science Academy, Lisbon/ Dagli Orti: 15, /University Museum, Cuzco/Mireille Vautier: 34tr, 119br. **Andrew McLeod:** 2, 3, 4bl, 4br, 5bl, 5bmr, 5br, 6tr, 23bl, 24tm, 25bm, 25br, 124tl, 124bl, 125bl, 126tl, 126br, 127br, 128.
Sally Phillips: 5bml, bl, 23bm, 24br, 100tr, 125tl. **Frances Reynolds:** 1, 23tr, 24bl, 25tm, 25bl, 44tr, 45tl, 66tr, 105tr, 123br, 127tl.
Nick Saunders: 2, 19tr, 24bm, 25tl, 33bl, 36bl, 56bl, 59bl, 60tr, 63tr, 68tr, 87tr, 115tl, 119t. **South American Pictures:** 10bl, 11bl, 12bl,

14bl, 29bl, 32tr, 34bl, 35tr, 37br, 38bl, 38tr, 39tr, 67tl, 70tr, 91tr, 105bl, 120bl, 122tr, /Danny Aeberhard: 51tr, /Ann Bailetti: 114tr, /Phillipa Bowles: 57t, / Hilary Bradt: 71, /Britt Dyer: 60bl, /Robert Francis: 46tr, 85bl, 89bm, 110tr, /Steve Harrison: 53bl, /Kathy Jarvis: 18tr, 20–1, 24tl, 31, 40–1, 42bl, 43tl, 54–5, 61br, 80tm, 80br, 81tl, 81br, 103bl, /Joseph Martin: 36tr, /Marion Morrison: 58tr, 99br, /Tony Morrison: 8–9, 12tr, 17bl, 17tr, 18bl, 19bl, 26-27, 28bl, 28tr, 30bl, 30tr, 32bl, 39b, 44bl, 45br, 45tr, 46bl, 47bl, 47tr, 48tr, 49bl, 50bl, 50tr, 51bl, 52bl, 56tr, 57br, 59tr, 62bl, 64tr, 65tr, 69, 83bl, 83br, 84bl, 85tr,

87bl, 88tr, 89t, 90bl, 94, 96tr, 98tr, 99tl, 101br, 104b, 108tr, 109br, 111t, 112tr, 113br, 114bl, 115br, 116bl, 117bl, 121, 122bl, /Peter Ryley: 65bl, /Chris Sharp: 62tr, 75br, 97, /Karen Ward: 53tr, 61tl.
Werner Forman Archive: 22tr, 120tr, /British Museum, London: 14tr, 66bl, 110bl, / Dallas Museum of Art, Dallas: 84tr, 85tl, /David Bernstein Collection, New York: 106-107, 108bl, 116tr, /Guggenheim Museum, New York: 52tr, /Maxwell Museum of Anthropology, Albuquerque, NM: 75bl, 76tl, /Museum fur Volkerkunde, Berlin: 17, 67br, 77tr, 98bl, 123tl, /Private Collection: 77bl.